Be Delusional

How I Manifested the Life of My Dreams.

By: Anna Rose Egres

Copyright © 2022 by Anna Rose Egres

All rights reserved. No part of this publication may be reproduced, distributed, or transmitted in any form or by any means, including photocopying, recording, or other electronic or mechanical methods, without the prior written permission of the publisher, except in the case of brief quotations embodied in critical reviews and certain other noncommercial uses permitted by copyright law.

For permission requests, write to the publisher, addressed "Attention: Permissions Coordinator," at the address below.

ISBN: 9798365290303

Alpha Book Publisher
www.alphapublisher.com

Ordering Information:

Quantity sales. Special discounts are available on quantity purchases by corporations, associations, and others. For details, contact the publisher at the address above.

For orders by U.S. trade bookstores and wholesalers, visit www.alphapublisher.com/contact-us to learn more.

Printed in the United States of America

Dedication

This book is dedicated to my father.

He was a very creative man and full of life.

It is also dedicated to anyone who is foolish enough to ignore society and believe that you can have whatever it is you want.

I am right there with ya. ☺

Table of Contents

Introduction *1*

Tell the Truth *5*

Rewriting Negative Programming *11*

Affirmations *23*

VISUALIZE *29*

Mornings are EVERYTHING *38*

The Same 24 Hours *42*

Write Down Clear & Concise Goals *50*

Scrapbook Your Space – *56*

Make a Massive Vision Board *56*

What Is It That You Want? *61*

Only Compare Yourself to Who You Were Yesterday *65*

Build Your House on Solid Rock, Leave the Sand Alone *70*

Negative Thoughts Are a Rabbit Hole *75*

Positive Thinking *80*

Have an Open Mind *88*

Taking Classes *94*

Give to Others *98*

Maslow's Hierarchy of Needs *104*

Is Your Work and Home Environment Stimulating Creativity? *113*

Critics & Their True Talents *118*

Be Disciplined *127*

Happiness *136*

Have Clear Set Boundaries *140*

The Power of "I Am" *144*

Be More in Love with Your Future Than Your Past *149*

Be Authentic – Be You *152*

Get a Mentor Coach *163*

Find One Person Who Believes in You More Than You Believe in Yourself *170*

No Time for Excuse *174*

Ask Why They Said, "No" *179*

Read – It's Where It's At *186*

It's All in Your Head *197*

Take Care of Your Body *203*

Your Energy *209*

4 Minute Mile *215*

Be Curious *217*

Use What You Believe In (Religious/Spiritual) To Help You Navigate Your Journey *219*

Daily Gratitude Lists 224

Make It Your Signature 235

It's Never Too Late 239

Write Your Goals Down! 242

Don't Let Anyone Tell You That You Can't Do Something! Where You Start is Not Where You are Going to End Up! 246

Birds of a Feather 255

Don't Focus on Your Fears, Focus on Your Desires 260

Be Careful How You Define Yourself! 263

Plan Everything 266

Procrastination Kills 268

Have Some Kind of Belief System 271

Play Tennis with a Better Player 277

Decide What It Is You Want & Accept Nothing Less 279

Get Quiet 281

Let Go of Control 282

Body Language 283

Say "When" Not "If" 285

My Grammy 287

Afterthoughts 288

Introduction

When I was only seven years old, I brought home from school a paper with the words, "Someday I am going to be a famous country music singer" and gave it to my mom. As I got older, I knew that statement was true, maybe not the country music part but the part that I would be a famous singer one day.

When I was 11 years old, I wrote my first "lyrical poem" (song without the chords) and tried performing it for my father poorly on his guitar. The song was about this boy I had a crush on in school who didn't like me because I was heavier than the other girls in our grade. After playing "Heavier set" for my father, he looked at me and said, "Sounds good, Banana. Just keep working on it." And even after my father passed away…that's what I did. I just kept working on it.

I was fortunate to know what I wanted to do with my life at such an early age. What my talents are and where my gifts lie. My sole purpose in life is to encourage/inspire/motivate people to go after their dreams through my songs, business endeavors, and everyday life. It is to let others know that they are not alone and that other people have had similar if not the same emotion as they are experiencing. There are no new problems. Whatever you are going through, someone has been through it before,

I guarantee it. Music has that ultimate healing power that is universal, and I have spent my entire life being obsessed with it.

I want everyone to know that I started writing this book on April 29th, 2019. I was not nominated for a Grammy. I never had my song on the radio. Never had won a songwriting contest. Didn't have a fan base. I was 26 years old. (Some people would probably say that's too old.) But there was a voice that was firm and steady deep down within my spirit, almost like a train, that told me if I just kept moving in the direction of my dreams someday, I would see them come to fulfillment. I don't know why but I just believed in it so strongly. I even changed my signature on my email to "Anna Maria Rose – Grammy Award Winning Singer/Songwriter." My mom emailed me back saying she was emailing a Grammy winner, probably thinking to herself, "my kid is nuts!"

When I was 23 years old, I moved to Nashville with no job and very little money in hopes of pursuing my dream. Some of my family members were upset and couldn't understand why I would leave my entire family in Michigan and move somewhere where I only knew one person. However, I researched famous musical artists and celebrities that I wanted to be like, and a lot of them moved to Nashville and found that their life changed following that move. Word going around town upon arriving was that Nashville had a 10-year plan and that most people didn't make it without putting in 10 years of hard work. I didn't care how long it took. I just wanted to see my musical dreams come to fruition.

I knew that there were things musically that I needed to work on. I was a little fish in a big pond. There were many musicians in town that vastly exceeded my technical skills (and probably still do) , but I don't know how many of them then or now have that burning desire and passion for music, as I do. It is the first thing I think about when I wake up and the last thing I think about before going to bed. And I don't think that will ever change. Music is the main topic of conversation for me. I am always sharing my knowledge with others and trying to gain more.

I always believed I was a Rockstar. I would dress like a Rockstar. Tell my friends I was a Rockstar. Walk and act like a fucking Rockstar. Be delusional enough to think you are deserving and worthy of your dreams and be crazy enough to hang in there long enough to get it.

Alpha Book Publisher

Tell the Truth

"Would you rather feel uncomfortable now or lie and have to face the music later? -Anonymous

If you want to make the most of your time and use it with the most efficiency. Lying is a complete waste of your time. Thomas J. Stanley, Ph.D., is the author of several books, but one, The *Millionaire Mind*, touches on the importance of telling the truth in our day-to-day lives. He says that for every one lie we tell, we must tell 15 more to cover up for that one lie! 15 more lies to make up for one! That's crazy! And then those 15 need another 15 each, so…you get the point. You find yourself in this big ball of lies, and it starts taking up your time.

I believe with everything in me, that what happens in the dark comes to light. Know that when you do something you have to lie to cover up, people will find out about it. You may even hurt someone you love or break their trust. And sometimes, when you break trust, you can't get it back. Think about what you are sacrificing when you lie. Would you rather feel uncomfortable now, or lie and have to face the music later? I'll take it now.

Remember the golden rule in business and your personal life. If you wouldn't want someone to do it to you, DON'T do it to them.

People like to do business with people they know, like, and trust. It is critical to your success that you become a person of good character. You want to be on a mission to become the best version of yourself rather than someone who lays awake at night worrying that their lies will be exposed. Get a good night's sleep and just tell the truth. It will save you so much time and heartbreak. I promise.

"Whoever is dishonest in a very little is dishonest also in much" (Luke 16:10)

What is being said here is, people who tell small lies inevitably are capable and willing to tell even bigger lies. If you see someone lacking in integrity or shows lapses in high moral character, if they don't receive punishment for these small acts of dishonesty, odds are it will snowball into something far greater later in life. It is important to be extra careful when we see people like this pop up in our own lives. If you find that this is you, please know that you're not lost. You can come back from that with a regular conscious awareness of honesty.

An article from the University of Notre Dame called *What Dishonesty Does to Your Brain* states that people who are more "prone to guilt" are more likely to lie. Ever noticed that you may lie to your spouse about eating the rest of the candy or about something that you're not particularly proud of? Therefore, telling the truth is always important, despite what we may or may not be feeling.

An article on Forbes.com states that Anita E. Kelly, a psychology professor at the University of Notre Dame had a foundation-funded research project called *The Science of Dishonesty*. The research that has been collected will surprise you. Kelly found that after taking 72 adults, dividing them into a control group and a "sincerity group" and giving the second group a strict mandate to only tell the truth for five weeks that they had fewer physical problems such as: headaches, sore throats and/or nausea than the other group that was not instructed to tell the truth. Also, they reported better overall mental health and fewer feelings of feeling tense. Lying causes stress and makes us more vulnerable to illness.

Know that even white lies aren't good for us. It is proven that we are more likely to tell these small white lies when we feel compassion. However, no matter how big or small, lies never benefit us in the long run. An article in the New York Times called *How Honesty Could Make You Happier* by Judi Ketteler in 2017 talks about a 2012 book by Dan Ariely called *The (Honest) Truth About Dishonesty*. The book states that we stretch the truth by about 10% and are more likely to lie when we think it will go undetected. It is also known that we are more likely to lie when we are around other people who lie. That probably has something to do with a mixture of feeling comfortable enough to lie and experiencing some peer pressure that we are not comfortable standing up to.

Not telling the whole truth is something I also consider lying. When you don't tell your customer things like there is a fee to clean up their logo or a service charge of 18 percent, some people can end up feeling bitter towards you because they believe you were trying to deceive them. Avoid this by being upfront with everyone and not leaving out pieces of information that they need to know that might impact them, their well being and/or their life.

Your Brain On Lying by Markham Heid states that within the first second of telling a lie, your brain releases cortisol, your heartbeat increases, you start to sweat, and your body goes into a fight or flight mode. Science tells us that when your body is in fight or flight mode, your immune system shuts down, and all your energy goes to fight off the perceived "predator". So, if lying sends you into fight or flight, it's shutting down your immune system and not fighting off harmful bacteria and viruses.

After five seconds, Markman explains that your memory is trying to recall exactly what you said to that person, so you will in the future be able to expand on the original story. Because of this, your ability to make wise decisions decreases. So, you start making dumber and dumber decisions. After ten, anger is said to rise within you towards the person you lied to. This anger presents itself so you can deflect your dishonesty onto the other person.

After 30 seconds, you may do one of two things, become sweet to the person you deceived or try to demonize and dominate them. Markman explains that you might even tell the person you lied to that they couldn't handle the truth. For people who lie regularly, 24 hours later, they start to act out/ become the lie and may treat the person they lied to differently simply because THEY lied. After three days, anxiety can result due to the lie, and your ability to think decreases. You are more likely to catch a cold due to your immune system not functioning at its highest. You could have trouble sleeping or falling asleep due to all the side effects that come with telling a lie. Please know that lying is not worth it. I, personally, would rather face the heat and get things out in the open, to begin with than to lie and must experience the ripple effects of the said lie.

Lying has consequences, and it's so much easier just to avoid them all by eliminating lies from your life.

Telling the truth builds solid relationships and allows people to know that they can trust you. Without truth, people will constantly be questioning whether you will do what you say and say what you do. People will have trouble learning to trust you again, and even when you are telling the truth, they may not believe you. You will feel extremely frustrated, and you will have no one to blame but yourself. You cried wolf and broke trust. And you will start having to prove yourself by walking in the light of truth and being patient with others as they allow you to regain their trust. Some people won't even tolerate people who lack integrity. Some people won't let you work to regain trust. So, it's crucial to be very careful. Don't damage your relationships, work, personal or otherwise so you can tell a lie. Others will follow that lie, and it's just not worth it!

Rewriting Negative Programming

"It's not the world against you, at all. The world will give you everything." -Dr. Bruce Lipton

"We can change the world we live in by just changing our thoughts, but that means changing the programming." -Dr. Bruce Lipton

That may be one of the hardest things you ever have to do. We have negative programs around; money, relationships.

There are multiple ways to reprogram. You are programmed from the last trimester of pregnancy until the age of six or seven. After that you can only be programmed in several ways. Those ways are as follows; repetition (practice), hypnosis, and energy psychology.

Bruce Lipton is an excellent person to read up on when it comes to reprogramming your mind. He is an American biologist and author of The Biology of Belief and The Honeymoon Effect and co-author of Spontaneous Evolution: Our Positive Future (And a Way to Get There from Here). I find what he has to offer very intriguing. He says that we are operating 95% of our day on automatic! Your subconscious mind programs 95% of your day. That means only 5% of your day you are consciously in control of! That's crazy! If you want to create lasting change in your life and make improvements, the small stuff isn't going to cut it. You must dig deep and work on yourself! You must make a commitment that you are going to rewrite all programs that hold you back from becoming the highest and most authentic expression of yourself!

One of the ways that we can reprogram our mind is through energy psychology. Psych-K is defined as "a set of principles designed to change subconscious beliefs that limit the expression of your full potential as a divine being having a human experience" and is one of the ways to reprogram using energy psychology and can take as little as 5 minutes.

When you are below the age of seven, you are observing, downloading, watching, and learning all the rules of how you conduct yourself in your society, culture, and religion. You watch your parents and pick up on their traits and habits.

You may not know it, but you could be doing self-destructive things unconsciously to help fulfill your programming. This is what, without you knowing it, can hold you back immensely.

Affirmations repeated are so unbelievably powerful! Many people, such as Les Brown and Bob Proctor, recite their goals multiple times daily and who they want to be. The trick is to say these things in the present tense and to REPEAT them. Repetition is one way in which we can override and rewrite negative programming. And it is entirely free! It is sort of like when you learned to drive a car. They didn't give you your license and say, have at it! No, you had to PRACTICE and take tests. Form good habits and repeat them and make things work for you!

You can also work on programming your mind with how you choose to use the time right before you fall asleep each night and right before you wake up. If you can listen to audio of how you wish your life to be and do that repeatedly, it can do wonders in your life. And you may not notice the positive changes right away but give it time because if you work it, it works!

You can also try hypnotherapy.

Something wonderful that I LOVE to do is to listen to positive money, success, and wealth affirmations at night when I sleep. What happens every night as you fall asleep and before you wake up is that you enter a state called Theta. Theta was the brain state that you were in the first seven years of your life. That was when you downloaded programs. That is the only time, past the age of six or seven, that we know of, that we are in Theta. So, you can start to override negative programming when you fall asleep and right before you wake up. I have several on my phone. But you can find lots of them on YouTube. And I try to select a time that works best for a time that I planned on sleeping; ex. 6 hours, 7.5 hours, 8 hours (preferred), or a 30 min cat nap. And this is so good. I usually feel that I sleep better, and my body is more well-rested when I wake up. Most of the time, when I listen to these positive affirmations while sleeping, overriding my negative programs, I wake up before any of my alarms go off, and wouldn't you know the program just ended or is ending.

Now, mind you, I am no doctor. So, I am only telling you what I know to be accurate based on my OWN experience. It is a great inexpensive way to override some of our negative programming, and almost all of us can do this. It's so easy. Your affirmations can be for anything, they don't have to be for wealth, money, or success. I just did that because that is where I seemed to be having troubles in my own life so I decided that was something I needed to work on. Look at the areas of your life where you find yourself constantly struggling and determine if there may be some harmful programs lurking in your subconscious mind that you may need to override.

These bad habits can stop with you. They don't have to be passed down to your children, grandchildren, and their children. I believe my negative programming around money and wealth has been passed down for generations. My grandpa was alive during the depression and was one of twelve. I'm sure food was scarce, and money was low. My family, as far as I've known, has been middle class. But we have some things that are taught to us that are holding us back. Now, don't get me wrong, I'm not saying that our parents or grandparents are evil people for programming our minds with negative things that would not serve us later in life. I am not saying that at all. I hope you know that your family and parents were doing the best they could with what they learned.

But this can stop with you. One of the areas that I struggled with was money, wealth, and success. I made a vow to myself that my children would grow up to be great with money. They will have knowledge and understanding. I will teach them how money is a tool for good and can do remarkable things and change lives rather than the mantra that "money doesn't grow on trees." When talking about rich people, I won't say something like, "how the other half lives." I won't describe money as evil or those who have it because I don't believe in that. And I think those things hindered my success in that area.

Circling back to listening to positive affirmations while you sleep. Please, talk to your doctor about how much sleep you should be getting yourself. And do your homework on the benefits of a good night's rest. I would highly suggest 8 hours. But I know some people will have objections to that suggestion, so I will advise you to do what is best for you.

One shocking statistic that I learned from Dr. Bruce Lipton is that stress causes 90% of doctor's visits. So, be aware of the pressures in your own life and how you can combat that to better serve you and your overall health. Stress hormones shut off your immune system. That alone makes me wonder if we, as a society, made general lifestyle changes that drastically reduced stress if we could drastically decrease the amount of illness in our community today. It is something to think about. I'm sure it could work if executed correctly.

Genes do not control your life! You are not a victim of your heredity! You can break cycles that have been in your family for generations! But it is up to you and your beliefs! There is something called Epigenetic Control and what that means is that your perception of your environment changes your genetic activity. Isn't that something? This no longer makes you a victim of your genes. You can change your environment and change your perception.

The mind is far more powerful than you can ever even begin to wrap your mind around. So, don't get stuck in stinkin' thinkin' and think things like, "Oh, I was born this way" or "Money is hard to come by" or "I'm gonna do what I have always done." No, you have the power to take charge of your own life, and you harness that power by taking control of your mind. Also, by watching the results, you are getting. If you like the results you are getting, they are because of your program. If you don't like the results that you are getting. They too are a result of your programming. Look at where you're at. Determine in what areas of your life that you are rocking out and what areas need assistance. If you don't do it, I can tell you right now that no one else will.

"How we live our lives is a result of the story we bought into." -Les Brown

Les Brown says that our thinking results from what we have been exposed to between the ages of zero and five. That is practically the same thing that Dr. Lipton is trying to tell the world. Both great men understand that we sometimes download programs that do not serve us and hold us back. Les used to work for this man before becoming a disc jockey and a motivational speaker. He said that one of the things that he loved most about him is his routine and the fact that he took time to work on reprogramming his mind every morning. Mr. Brown claimed that he used to listen to Earl Nightingale recordings and others with successful men sharing their wisdom on becoming a success.

"All of us are self-made, but only the successful will admit it." -Earl Nightingale

"People form habits, and habits create futures." -Denis Waitley

"If you give enough people what they want, they will give you what you want." -Zig Ziglar

"When the end comes for you, let it find you conquering a new mountain, not sliding down an old one." -Jim Rohn

"The truth is incontrovertible. Malice may attack it, ignorance may deride it, but in the end, there it is." -Winston Churchill

These are things you must let seep into your mind. These things help you create a grander vision for your life than the one you had before. Find recordings and teachings such as these and listen to them over and over and over! Les Brown calls people who go through life stuck because of negative thoughts and programming that don't do anything about it "Volunteer Victims." That is what you are if you don't take the necessary actions to change your life when we have so many tools at our aid to help mold and shape us into the highest, truest expression of ourselves!

Les Brown also says that some people may die an early death but continue to live. These people are not technically dead, but they have given up on their dreams, hopes and goals. They are dead before they reach the graveyard. Live every day with hunger and an aliveness to go after your deepest desires. Mr. Brown claims that the richest place in the world is the graveyard. Their dreams, ideas, inventions, businesses, etc. that were given to individuals to bring forth, to give birth to, died with them instead of coming to pass, and being of service to the world. He always asks his audiences what dreams will die with them? That is most certainly something for you to think about!

"You can walk outside and find pigeons but if you look for eagles, it's gonna take you a minute" that's another saying by Les Brown that just proves to us that being "extraordinary isn't average. If you want to raise your standards and live a higher quality of life you are going to have to change many things about yourself and how you live. You may not be able to have the same lifestyle, engage in the same activities, or hang with the same people you used to. This is where the sacrifice comes in.

Brendon Burchard says to ask positive questions and answer them multiple times a day to start to shift the thoughts in your mind. If you look for ways to be grateful or surprise and delight someone, you begin to focus on good things and not on things of the opposite nature. Another idea of his that I like is thinking about three words that you would like to define you and make them pop up as notifications on your phone throughout the day. This is great because it allows you to check yourself and see if you are genuinely working on what you say you want.

Tony Robbins has said that to become the success we see him as today, he had to "sculpt" his body and mind. Most people are not born with the programming they need to succeed, get ahead in life, and become the highest version of themselves. It requires a lot of work and being mindful of who you are and who you want to be. Tony said that he practiced incantations to help shape his mind. "So, an incantation is not only how you speak it, but you embody what you are saying with all the intensity that you can. And you do it with enough repetitions that it sticks in your head." To simplify it, an incantation is an affirmation amplified and on crack.

You can do incantations in your car or in your house. You may not want to try to do them in front of too many people. You may receive some funny looks if you do but if you are okay with that, go at it by any means. That is not just a saying to change the programming of your mind. It's something that changes your energy and changes your physical state. It is so important to change your energy. When you get to that high-flying state, more and more good things will be attracted to you, and your brain will start getting addicted to that reward of the high-flying state. It will want to repeat the action, and therefore you will experience better and more good energy.

Keep a clean house. Keep your desk clean at work or in your office space. That is important because if you see chaos and clutter in your environment it will manifest in your life, too. When you have a clean environment, you feel as if everything has a place, and you feel in control. It also forces you not to be lazy and leave things undone. I have a friend whom I call "Mom" (even though she is not my mom), and she says that it is crucial to keep clean sinks and to make your bed daily. At first, I had to try to hold myself accountable for doing this. Now, it's become a habit for me to make my bed and keep my sinks clean and empty. If I don't, I feel chaotic and feel a slight loss of control. It's weird to admit. But I will tell you that if you try it, you WILL see the benefits! Be clean and be orderly.

Welcome plants into your home! It will do wonders in improving your happiness and creativity. Help plant a tree or plant a garden. Pull the weeds in your garden and pluck negative thoughts and negative programming from your mind!

Evan Carmichael believes that a key to changing your mind is changing your environment, as I said before. The people around you influence who you are. He provides an excellent example of how your environment shapes you. If you want to be an entrepreneur and your parents have been employees their entire lives, odds are they will be programming you with an employee mindset and not the mentality of a boss or an entrepreneur. Your new environment will help shape who you will be.

Reading books, attending seminars, courses, classes, or watching online videos of successful and innovative people will either continue to reinforce your positive mental thoughts and programs that are pre-existing, or it will open the door to a different way of being that you never even knew existed. Once you immerse yourself in this environment and expose yourself to a way of life that expands rather than shrinks who you are. It is not enough to do it once! You must continually do this and make it a part of your daily life until it becomes normal for you! Doing this daily will help to engrain the proper program you need to help you live your best life!

Affirmations

"Whatever we plant in our subconscious mind and nourish with repetition and emotion will one day become a reality." —Earl Nightingale

I know I touched on the power of affirmations in other parts of this book. But I can't just stress enough how important they are.

Bob Proctor teaches us to say, "I am so happy and grateful now that…" and follow it with what you wish to manifest in your life and repeat it to yourself multiple times a day with enthusiasm. For all you cynics out there, try it and believe it, and it will work for you as well. Affirmations are potent and can be used to correct areas of our lives that need improvement.

Your Youniverse Channel on YouTube describes an affirmation as "a statement of truth consciously used to become the directing power of life's expression. Only he can who thinks he can. The world makes way for only the determined man, for the man who laughs at barriers, limits others, at stumbling blocks over which others fall."

The channel also says, "Confidence is the father of achievement." By using affirmations, we begin building confidence and stating that life is different from our current reality. That's where the law of attraction comes in. You don't get in life exactly what you want. We get in life what we are and attract, what is vibrating at the same energy level we are. So, if you don't like what is going on in your life, look at the level you're vibrating on. What you put out into the universe comes back to you.

Use affirmations to start changing your life. Perhaps you have been involved with driving accidents, and your insurance is sky-high. Your affirmation could be, "I am a safe and responsible driver." Perhaps you are always running late and are ill-prepared. Your affirmation could be, "I'm always a little early for all events, parties, and meetings. I always come prepared."

Start seeing yourself living the life you say you so desperately want. Say your affirmations out loud, read and write them multiple times a day. Know that you don't have to stay where you are.

"Hitch your wagon to a star." – Ralph Waldo Emerson

When writing affirmations, make sure they are always written and spoken out loud in the present tense. You don't want to say, I will. Although that sounds good. You want to say, "I am."

When I was a little girl, I made the mistake of writing my affirmations with "I will" instead of

"I am." I simply did not know any better. On my dresser at my parents' house to this day, you can probably still find that small piece of stationery that says, "Someday, I will be famous." "Someday, I will have a Grammy(s). Notice the 'S'." I was a determined child with big dreams. Some days I still feel like that child. Even though I am an adult now, I still have those big dreams, and I must find ways to achieve my dreams, little by little, day by day.

Affirmations are a great way to start to alter your behavior, what you expect of yourself, and who you see yourself as. I used to run late for a lot of things, school, work, you name it. I started saying to myself, "I am always on time." And what do you know, it worked. Most of the time, I can honestly say that I am on time, if not early. I have been to interviews before where I am there, even before the interviewers! When you do show up early, people take notice!

The confidence you receive from affirmations will improve your energy and make you overall feel more powerful! Affirmations are used to challenge or change negative thoughts and beliefs we have about ourselves. Doing this, in turn, over time, changes our overall outcomes. Positive affirmations help to motivate us and boost our self-esteem and help define us.

When we start to see changes in our self-esteem, motivation, and confidence, our ability to solve problems and navigate our hardships becomes easier.

In an article by positive psychology.com, they list the benefits of daily affirmations. They are as follows:

1. Self-affirmations have been shown to decrease health-deteriorating stress (Sherman et al., 2009; Critcher & Dunning, 2015);
2. Self-affirmations have been used effectively in interventions that led people to increase their physical behavior (Cooke et al., 2014);
3. They may help us to perceive otherwise "threatening" messages with less resistance, including interventions (Logel & Cohen, 2012);
4. They can make us less likely to dismiss harmful health messages, responding instead with the intention to change for the better (Harris et al., 2007) and to eat more fruit and vegetables (Epton & Harris, 2008);
5. They have been linked positively to academic achievement by mitigating GPA decline in students who feel left out at college (Layous et al., 2017);
6. Self-affirmation has been demonstrated to lower stress and rumination (Koole et al., 1999; Weisenfeld et al., 2001).

Affirmations are known to increase optimism and resilience in those that make them a daily practice.

I couldn't have a chapter in my book on affirmations without mentioning Louise Hay. She was a motivational author and the founder of Hay House. She authored the book *Heal Your Body* in 1976. In her teen years, she was abused, and in her adult years, she beat cancer without surgery or drugs. She used affirmations, visualization, nutritional cleansing, and psychotherapy. In 1984, she came out with a book called, *You Can Heal Your Life*. She believed that our ideas and beliefs about ourselves could help or hurt us.

You can find her affirmations online. When I listen to them, I feel at peace, stronger, more powerful, and more in love with life. For years you could find her 365-day calendar of daily affirmations on my desk. I believe that she has helped mold me and presented new ways of thinking that have helped me become the person I am today.

You can find positive affirmations online for any dilemma you are having or any age you might be. Using these affirmations to our advantage and reaping the benefits of what they offer will alter the course of your life!

Like the picture on the box of a puzzle, affirmations help us know where we are going.

Without a clear picture, our inner definition of ourselves would remain the same.

Marisa Peer, speaker, therapist, and bestselling author, believes in one affirmation that will outdo the rest. She says that most people don't feel as if they are enough. If you feel inadequate in any way, shape, or form, please, check out her teachings. You can find her on YouTube or at marispeer.com or check out one of her many books. Say to yourself, "You are enough." She encourages you (so I did) to write it on your bathroom mirror. I also programmed it on my phone. Once at 8 a.m. and once at 10 p.m. I had one of my friends do it too. But she became nervous about what people would think of her, and she stopped. Don't let what people think stop you. GO BOLDLY IN THE DIRECTION OF YOUR DREAMS!

VISUALIZE

"What you imagine, you create." —Buddha

"Imagination is more important than knowledge. For knowledge is limited, whereas imagination embraces the entire world, stimulating progress, giving birth to evolution." -Albert Einstein, What Life Means to Einstein (1924)

"Thoughts become things. If you see it in your mind, you will hold it in your hand." – Bob Proctor, You Were Born Rich.

Five minutes a day of imagining yourself in the role you want, overcoming obstacles, having the positive mental attitudes you want, etc., can have a lasting positive impact and generate healthy emotions. You have absolutely nothing to lose by spending at least 5 minutes a day visualizing the life you want! The best part is, it's free!

When you start to visualize and practice your affirmations daily, there will be some tension created in your brain. It's going to realize that what you're saying and visualizing is not in line with your current reality. That will cause a shift in your perception, and because of this, you will become more creative, and be more aware of opportunities when they come your way. And you will have a fire inside like you have never known. That will cause you to move on to those opportunities that you are stumbling on and, in return, get you closer to reaching the goal that you have been visualizing and doing affirmations about. This stuff works. I promise you, it does.

There is a song I wrote called *Changes Faces Like the Moon,* and I would love the country duo The Brothers Osborne or the talented Mr. Chris Stapleton record. When I first had this desire, you must know, it seemed merely impossible for me to wrap my head around. It seemed so farfetched. I did something only someone who is genuinely DELUSIONAL would do. I photoshopped a picture of me onto a picture of The Brothers Osborne. I know that seems crazy, but someday, when they record my song, it won't be. I did this because looking at it every day on my bathroom door tricked my brain and made me look at it like it was just another picture of me with some friends. That took them off their pedestal and made them more human to me. So, when I meet them one day and they record my song, I won't treat them like one of Elvis's screaming fans would. That is something I used as a technique to help me visualize the desired future for myself.

Because that seemed to work for me, I did the same with British-American musician, DJ, songwriter, and record producer Mark Ronson. He has worked with some big names, and I love and admire his work. In a spirit of hopefulness that he will someday work with me, I made a fake flyer of the two of us, announcing that we were working on an album together, and it hangs on my closet door. Mark, if you are reading this, let's work together!

I also went as far as looking up blank images of Forbes Magazine covers and inserting my picture and the month in which I desire to be featured (it's September if you were wondering). I was told one time to take off my rose-colored glasses and join the rest of the people. And I hate to break it to all the naysayers out there, but I enjoy my glasses.

Dr. Myles Munroe had a list of things that your vision will dictate once you discover it. The list is as follows:

1. Your Future
2. Your Friends
3. Your Library
4. Your Use of Time
5. Your use of Energy
6. Your Movies
7. Your Priorities in Life
8. Your Hobbies
9. The Games You Play
10. Your Diet
11. How You Invest Your Money
12. How You Write Your To-Do List
13. Your Attitude in Life
14. Your Life

15. Your Life's Plan – How to plan your living
16. Your Values

That is something that most people don't even think about. And I'm sure I may have missed one in there, but you get the point.

"Vision makes you believe in things that you have no money to pay for." -Dr. Myles Munroe

That is truly remarkable. Vision will take you out of your current situation, out of your current economic class, and transport you to a world and a way of being beyond your wildest dreams. It gives you faith to call forth things that don't exist but soon will. When you have a clear vision, it will continue to internally motivate you to become the highest and truest expression of yourself!

Vision creates and attracts resources, Myles said. He made it clear that people don't give to people; they give to a vision. So, perhaps you need funding to get your project off the ground. Maybe you are too focused on what people think of you and not focused enough on what people think about your vision. It needs to be clear and well-defined. Often, dreams and visions are given to us to solve problems and help to alleviate suffering. Therefore, people buy into vision. The vision is what people sign up for. Make your vision plain. So, anyone you tell your vision to can begin to see it too.

Your destiny determines your friends. Dr. Myles Munroe defined a friend as "anyone who is willing and committed to help you get to your destiny." Now, that might mean that they won't always tell you what you want to hear. When you fall off course, a friend will be there to say, you know I think that what you're doing now is not in your best interest, or they will say, I think that's a great opportunity, but I think it may distract you from your overall goal. And noticed that he said, *committed!* There is nothing legally binding this person to you, but they are committed to you, nonetheless. They are not going to give up on you when you make mistakes or experience setbacks. They will be there to support you and help to guide you in the right direction. Very important.

"So, if you wanna be great, don't keep company with small-minded people. If you wanna be a success, stay away from failures." -Dr. Myles Munroe

Your friends should stimulate your dreams. He said that anyone who doesn't, he would describe it as pollution. You must have the strength and the know-how to stay away from dream killers and people who try to squash your dreams. Sometimes these people are your family, and that doesn't make them bad people. It just makes them people that you don't need to be spending most of your time with. Be with people who lift you up, who remind you of your dream, and people who see more significant potential in you than you see in yourself. That will help you to plant good seeds in your mind about who you are and where you are going!

Also, you want to surround yourself with people who stretch you. I've often heard it said that if you are the smartest one in your group of friends, you should probably get a new group. Be with people who not only stimulate your vision but stimulate your mind. Surround yourself with people you can learn from and people who will teach you new and exciting things. Maybe they are older and wiser than you, or avid readers and are constantly dropping knowledge and telling you about great books. You want to be around people that you can ask questions and receive different solutions to your problems. Be around people who can expand your mental growth!

Myles said that vision is the next best thing to time travel and that it means being slightly spaced out. It allows you to see a more expansive reality. It gives you the courage to take risks. Vision gives you faith that what you see in your mind will soon, in fact, come to pass. He said that vision will make you believe in a better world. And knowing that, why would you not allow vision to help mold and shape you into becoming your highest, truest version of yourself.

People who have vision are incredibly passionate, and they are not living in the past. They understand the importance of being conscious and living in the present, but they see and focus on where they are going! When I was younger, I took horseback riding lessons, and learned to always be looking where you want to go! The same is valid with people! If you are concentrating on your problems, you will simply manifest more problems. If you focus on the future that you would like to manifest and your dreams, hopes, and vision for a better tomorrow and for the years to come, you will begin to manifest that of the like. Just pretend you are riding your horse, focus on the space between their two ears, and extend your vision outward from there to something in the distance! It is so important to keep the vision alive of where you are going instead of where you have been!

Get positioned in a way when you free yourself from distractions and noise! God/The Universe (whatever name you use) speaks to you when you get quiet and will give you directions, guidance, and subtle whispers on how to achieve the vision that has been planted in your heart. Without the stripping away of everyday distractions, it can be hard to reach you!

Dr. Myles Munroe said that "Meditation is the most important aspect of prayer." Prayer is when you do the talking but meditation is more for listening and most of us have no problem talking to our higher power and asking for all the things in our life that we want and think we need. But we don't spend much time *listening*. Don't get me wrong, I am not saying I'm a meditation expert. But I am working on making time each day to meditate and try to clear my thoughts of all the clutter, focus on my breathing, and make myself open for the creator/my higher power to speak to me.

"Let me tell you; your dream is never revealed to you while you are talking. And we think prayer is talking." -Dr. Myles Munroe

Spend more time listening from here on out. See if you get that guidance and wisdom from the source speaking to you in the time you are listening. He said to think of it like a friend that you go to with a problem, and you are talking to them, wanting their advice, but after you get done explaining the situation, you just get up and leave. That is why he claims that there cannot be prayer without meditation. One is talking, and one is listening.

Vision is the thing that won't leave you, said Myles. It hangs around for 30 or 40 years or more and may have started when you were ten or younger. For some of you, you may have been confused about what the vision for your life was, and now you may be thinking, *oh, it's that passion I have for ___ that I keep coming back to!* As I said, I knew that music would be a major part of my life since the age of seven. Now, I don't know to what degree that will be. But I know my songs and my voice are part of a larger vision for my life.

Sometimes your vision will be a solution to something that angers or upsets you. Perhaps, seeing people living on the streets makes you livid. You know that there are plenty of resources for everyone to have the necessities, and possibly your vision is eradicating homelessness by starting shelters in major cities. For me, one thing that upsets me is a lot of music nowadays that lacks substance. My vision for my music is always to create and contribute music and songs that have depth, and people can relate to on a deeper level, not just a surface level.

Proverbs 29:18 King James Version (KJV)

18 Where there is no vision, the people perish: but he that keepeth the law, happy is he.

We need vision to keep us going, to keep us striving to become more, better, and the best we can be. With a lack of vision, we become unmotivated and complacent with where we are at. And our creator (whatever name you call the creator: The Universe, God, Allah, Yahweh, etc.) does not want you to become complacent! It's such a miracle that you were born and that you are here now! You were given talents and hope and dreams for a reason. The creator wants you to create and alleviate suffering in people's lives the best way you know-how!

Mornings are EVERYTHING

"How you start your day is how you live your day."
-Kristine Carlson

If you never heard him speak about it, take some time and check out what Tony Robbins calls *The Hour of Power,* 20 minutes of prayer/meditation, 20 minutes of exercise, and 20 minutes of reading. When it comes to reading, it's essential that this reading that you do inspires you and does not depress you. Find material that will provide the best service to you when it comes to that.

Many Millionaires and Billionaires get up 3 hours before they start their workday. That is crucial. So, if your workday starts at 8:30, get up at 5:30. Take that time to read, meditate, pray, plan your day, etc. Whatever it is that will help you gain control over your day, do that. You want to go into everyday life with clarity, intention, and the power to take charge of your day instead of it taking control of you.

Eric Thomas, ET, the hip-hop preacher, will be the first one to tell you that there is "no alarm clock needed, my passion wakes me." Since I started listening to him in my college years and buying and reading his books, I have found him a source of great inspiration. Perhaps, it's because we are both from Michigan, I don't know. After listening to ET, I found myself questioning if I needed an alarm to wake me up or would my body wake me up just like he said it would? Well, it turns out Eric Thomas is right, yet again. Try it when you go to bed tonight. State clearly to yourself what time you intend on waking up, and believe it or not, you will wake up at that time, feeling refreshed and ready to start your day. Your brain is a miraculous thing, and so is the body. Use it to help you become the highest version of yourself. Get up and start your day.

Don't roll out of bed and immediately react and immediately respond to everyone on social media and all the notifications on your phone. That doesn't set you up for success! Take some time in the morning before you let everyone and their brother have access to your precious time to be mindful about how you want to start and go about your day. Set intentions for your day. And prioritize three to six things that you need to get done that day to advance you towards your goals and dreams.

Then focus on the one most important thing that you need to do that day and make sure you can get it done. Mel Robbins has this thing where she says that you should plan an ending time to your day. It's essential to decide when you will be done with work and your hobbies and being "on-call" for whoever wants to get in contact with you and just be present in your home with your family. I think this is something that you can plan out in your mornings too.

Working out in the morning is a great way to start your day and to wake yourself up. When you do highly intense workouts, you allow your body to release cortisol, the stress hormone. That can enable you to approach your day in a way that is more likely to succeed because you will be less stressed, and the odds are that when you encounter stress, you will be more likely to deal with it in a healthier manner. So, getting out and getting active in the morning is a great way to start your day.

Keep in mind that you are not going to always feel like it, and you are going to want to hit the snooze button and get that extra 7-15 minutes or half an hour of sleep. Let me tell you, I struggle with this myself. I fall prey to hitting the snooze but I'm actively working on mastering the art of not hitting the snooze because every time I don't, I get up early and get going, and start my mornings in healthy, productive ways, I FEEL BETTER. And you can feel better too. Start working out in the mornings and get it out of the way, so you don't even have to worry about it the rest of the day.

People say to try to rise before the sun daily, and your life will change because you are changing!

And I believe it. Don't let your mornings be chaotic, hectic, stressful, or negative because it will find its way to creep into the rest of your day. Find healthy, productive, beneficial, and purposeful ways that set you up for mental, spiritual, emotional, and physical growth. Practices will help you adapt and change and evolve and get into better shape in all areas of your life.

The Same 24 Hours

"Discipline is the whole key to being successful. We all get 24 hours each day. That's the only fair thing; it's the only thing that's equal. What we do with those 24 hours is up to us." -Sam Huff

    I guess this would fall under the same category as "No excuses" but I really feel like this deserves its own special section. I am just going to put this out there…" OPRAH HAS THE SAME 24 HOURS AS YOU." Let that sink in. Did I hurt your feelings? If I did, I'm not sorry. Oprah has the same 24 hours as you. You don't need more time. You need to use that time more wisely.

    I guess this could go under the part I've written about planning. But seriously, have you ever heard of time management? Don't tell me you don't have time to work out or don't have time to work on that novel you have always wanted to write! So, are you going to tell me that the hot guy at the gym with the really nice abs, who works two jobs has more time than you...? I'll wait.

    Didn't think so.

    Stop telling yourself that you don't have time for all these things that you want or need to do to better your life! Just do them! I know you aren't always going to feel like it but no one always feels like it. And news flash, we know you're lying! And we know you are just a cop out! Gig is up!

Some successful people plan their days down to five- or six-minute intervals. Try doing that and then try to talk to me about how you don't have time to accomplish whatever dream or goal you are aiming at.

A lot of us take time to educate ourselves on money management, business management, and other ways of controlling our resources and our environment but we don't always take the time to learn about and work on our time management skills.

Parkinson's Law states that "work expands so as to fill the time available for its completion."

So, now that you know this, do better. Make sure you take the time to block out your day. Plan how much time you are going to spend on one activity. Plan how much time you will spend on one task. Plan how much time it will take you to write that paper or finish that proposal. Don't fall prey to procrastination. Don't get skilled at talking yourself out of things.

Plenty of us know that if we have a week to complete a task for our boss and if we are given 2 days we can make the task last both time frames. If you can get your work done in a shorter amount of time, why not? You will have more time to spend with family and friends or on hobbies and other activities that you may enjoy.

Be very careful how you spend your time and who you are spending your time with. Time is one of our most precious resources. Once it is gone we cannot get it back. Material objects we can replace. However, time is something that we cannot replace so it is crucial that you are using it to be productive and live a balanced life that allows you to have the most success in most areas.

Just remember the homeless man on the corner and the billionaire are given the same 24 hours in a day. Their circumstances and background are, no doubt, different but their amount of time given to them at the beginning of every single day is the same. Use your time to do good things and improve the lives of others.

Make sure you don't waste your time doing things that you are not good at or that you don't like. Make sure you are not wasting your time doing something that someone else would be more than happy to do. For example, you can hire landscapers to keep your lawn and flowers looking in tip-top shape. You can hire cleaners to clean your house, so you spend more time reading, with your family, working on your career or doing something else you love. Perhaps, if you have children you can assign them daily, weekly and monthly chores to help lighten your load and help free some time up so that it can be spent on other things.

Do the thing that you don't want to do first, whether that means you have to fire someone at work, talk to your boss about considering you for that raise, give your presentation, record that video. Whatever it is, do it and get it out of the way. You don't want the stress of it looming over you and affecting your productivity for the rest of the day.

Take advantage of online calendars, wall calendars, desk calendars, and planners. Use all of them or use whatever is best for you but make sure you know your schedule and make sure you know what it is that you are doing day in and day out. If you don't plan your life, someone else will do it for you!

Probably one of the hardest things for me to learn is how to say "no." And I know that later on in the book, I mention how you should eliminate that word for your vocabulary, but I guess this is the exception to the rule. You cannot give everyone and everything, your precious time and energy. You need time to rest and refuel. You need to spend quality time with the people you love, and you need to spend time doing things that you love that fill your heart with joy. It's okay to say, "no" and turn down offers that don't serve you or offers to do things that get in the way of the things in your life that you have ranked, a higher priority.

Make sure your time means something and that you don't just give it away to anyone or anything. The rich know what a valuable resource time is. And it's time for everyone to know it too.

People are not going to hate you because you turned down their latest invitation to see the current *Star Wars* movie for a third time in theatres. Just know that the world isn't going to combust just because you decline someone's offer. It's okay to say "no" from time to time and prioritize your time in a way so that you get the maximum results.

Another thing that you can do is rid your mind from the idea that everything you do has to be perfect. I would have never embarked on the journey of writing this book, if I let the fear of it not being perfect stop me. Of course, it's not going to be perfect. It's my first book. I would expect it not to be perfect and be shocked if it was. Don't let the need for perfection keep you from starting tasks and/or getting them done.

Think about all the time you waste waiting in line or waiting for the nurses to come out the door with their clipboards and finally call your name for your doctors' appointment. How about the time you waste just waiting for your food at a restaurant, if you are dining by yourself? How could you use that time more efficiently? Perhaps you could take your laptop or tablet and get a little work done. Perhaps you could take that time to read novels, non-fiction, or articles from scholarly journals or magazines. Or maybe you could take that time to brainstorm how to take your business to the next level. Are you beginning to see just how much time we waste?

Your weekly commute in your car could be used to further your education. Your car could become a university. Take audio books that interest you or in areas that specialize in what you struggle in and gain knowledge while you are making a commute. Instead of listening to a radio show and jabber about bad hookups and what-would-you-do-if you could be getting an equivalent to an associates degree simply by listening to audiobooks while in your car as you make your daily commute over the time period of several years. How could you use that information to better your business, your marriage and your mental game? It's so easy to do these types of things yet, some of us still fail to execute. It's okay if you have failed in the past when it comes to this but that doesn't mean you have to keep failing.

If you must run errands, run your errands in a way that makes the most efficient use of your time. Map it out before you leave. Don't go to the grocery store without a list. If you go with a list, it will be a quicker trip and it will cost less, and odds are that you won't end up forgetting something that you needed. If you need to do housework, make a list of what you must do and go at it! Plan your children's after school activities in a way in which you can optimize your time. Maybe you can benefit from cooking on Sunday and prepping your meals in advance and label the food container with a day and who they are for. Get creative and search for answers on how you can maximize your time. It might even mean having groceries and other goods delivered to your doorstep.

    Also, when you are doing something, just do that. If you are working on writing a book, put your phone in the other room. You don't want notifications, texts and calls distracting you. You will end up with a half-written sentence with no idea how to finish it. When you are eating dinner with your family, be present. Don't be on your phone sending work emails. Reason number one being you will feel like you're stretched too thin and you must be two places at once. Reason number two being, your family might not think that you value them and could develop thoughts and feelings of resentment.

    So, get the most out of your time. Prioritize the things in life that are important to you and make sure to make time for those things. Get creative. Seek answers to time management dilemmas. You aren't the only mom out there who struggles to get her kids to bed on time and clean up the kitchen before going to bed. And lastly, don't forget to delegate, make lists, plan and block out your time.

If we can manage our finances and our businesses, then we can manage our time, too.

Write Down Clear & Concise Goals

"People who write down their goals earn 9 times as much over their lifetime as people who don't." - *Professor David Kohl, Virginia Tech*

People who just think about their goals have a 43% success rate. People who write their goals down have a 56% success rate and people who think, write and share with a friend have a 64% success rate. People who do all of this and share a weekly progress report with a friend have a 76% success rate. These numbers are based on a study done by Dr. Gail Matthews of Dominican University.

Knowing this alone, makes you INSANE not to do these 4 small things. Those things are so easy to do and just look at how much they help. I love having a friend to share a weekly progress report to. I do that and I didn't even know that statistic until I sat down to write this book. It's truly remarkable.

Sharing the work you have done or not done all week ties into another thing that I mention a little later in the book, that is who you hang out with.

Make sure they are holding you accountable and not stunting your growth.

The Canfield Training Group says that you should write down your "Top 5 Priority Action Steps you need to take every day to achieve your most important goal." I do this, as well. If you ever sell Mary Kay Cosmetics, they will teach you to do something of the like. Every morning, I write down between 3 and 5 things that I can do that day that will bring me closer to achieving my goal. I think the longer the list gets, personally, the harder it is for me to achieve. So, maybe start by dipping your feet into this and start with a couple action steps. You will start to gain momentum when you realize baking the pie isn't as daunting of a task if you can just follow a recipe step by step.

"Progress equals happiness." -Tony Robbins. The progress you make on the journey to achieving the worthy goal will give you immense happiness. The satisfaction from achieving the goal won't last forever. It is important to always have something you are aiming at, no matter how young or old you are or what line of work you are in.

When many people think of goal setting, they think of making S.M.A.R.T. goals.

Dr. Myles Munroe said, "Write all of your desires down on paper," he said, "You might end up with 10 pages. Don't be alarmed." Write all your desires down and worry about simplifying them later. It's important to know the desires that are in your heart. If you haven't taken the time to write your desires down prior to reading this book, take some time to do that now.

Trust and have faith that your desires, that are in your heart, will be given to you in time. Believe in it like a child. Law of attraction can be explained, in a way, like ordering pizza at a restaurant. When you order your pizza the server goes away, puts your order in with the kitchen, the kitchen works on your pizza and your server brings it to you when it's done. Don't ever think that the desires and dreams of your heart are anything different. They were put there for a reason and will come to you with divine timing if you can let go and stop focusing on them not being here. Know that what is meant for you will be yours in time! It is on its way to you!

There are six things that Dr. Munroe made clear regarding vision and how it should be translated to paper. The first is that your vision should be simple and clear. The second is that he asked that we write all our desires down on paper. Thirdly, he told us that, ""Your goal is to get your entire life's purpose in one sentence." Reduce your life to one sentence is what he would say. I think of it like a mission statement for a company but instead, that mission statement is for you and your life. He said that many people are willing and want to help us navigate the twists and turns in life but if they don't know who you are, what you are doing or where you are going that gets kind of hard to do.

"My purpose in life is to use my voice and my songs to change people's lives for the better." I could go on into further detail but that is my one sentence. It's important to know what your one sentence is, and have it written clearly and displayed somewhere where you see it regularly. I put mine on the top corner of my bathroom mirror.

"Identify your gifts and talents and summarize them in one sentence. To the point where you know, this is who and what I am. This is what I bring to the world. This is what I give to the world. This is what I offer my generation. This is me and this is what they need from me. That's your vision in life. You need to capture that in one sentence." -Dr. Myles Munroe

Step four is to communicate that single sentence to others. Put it on a brochure or a plaque, he says. Step five is to make a plan based on that sentence. This is where you begin to make a roadmap of the action steps you need to take to get to where you're going. "Plan is your strategy to get to your vision," he says. Don't skip the plan. Next up is, as you go along you need to take time to REVISE your vision. This step is really important because Dr. Munroe says you must go back and revise, revisit your original vision and see if you are on course. You may need to adjust some things.

This is where it gets tricky. That's where I think so many of us go wrong. We are too afraid of failing or making a mistake or how others might perceive us if we do something out of our norm or try something new. Provide something for adjustment! That's so important. I would rather you take the wrong action and have to change course than take no action, at all. And I speak for myself too on this one. I've had to revise my vision and I have also been guilty of lacking action in which to readjust.

Finally, evaluate your vision. "Evaluating your vision means that you keep judging yourself. Am I doing what I say I was born to do? Or am I getting off track?" -Dr. Myles Munroe

What comes to my mind when I think about evaluating my vision and seeing if somewhere I've fallen terribly off track is swimming with my family at our lake house in Michigan. At night or in the morning when you can either no longer or before you can make wake, a bunch of us will swim across the lake and back. The only time I find myself completely off track and using force to swim in a direction I don't want to go in, is when I'm not looking where I am going. It happens when I am not focused on my final destination. And someone may outswim me to shore not because they are a better swimmer than me or I am better than them, it's simply a matter of focus. Here I am exerting all this energy and I'm not going in a straight line like I think I am, I am swimming diagonally and away from my perceived target. Therefore, it takes me longer to get back to our lake house. That's why evaluating your vision is so important. Don't let yourself get off track for too long. You'll miss out on where you are going.

Suggestions from Dr. Myles Munroe:

1. Your greatest enemy is distraction.
2. Your greatest distraction is not bad things, but good things. The greatest distraction to your vision is not doing bad things but, what? Good things.
3. Vision comes in phases. It is given in phases and fulfilled in phases. What you are doing now, you might not be doing in ten years. This may just be a phase of the vision, a part of it.

Scrapbook Your Space

—

Make a Massive Vision Board

"You can't be what you can't see." -Marian Wright Edelman

I know what you are thinking. She probably is getting endorsed by the post-it notes companies or Staples or Office Depot to say this. WRONG! But what I do know is for years my apartment was a haven of positivity. Every time I came home, I was uplifted and inspired. I lined my bathroom mirror with Grammy Award Winning singers like Amy Winehouse, Adele and Beyoncé. I lined my mirror with quotes I found compelling from the bible and The Wife of Noble Character parable from the bible. I put quotes from books I read that motivated me and compelled me to do something different with my life. I posted affirmations to trick myself out of giving into my fears and remind me that it is possible for me to live the life that I desire.

People would come over and they would be amazed that positivity blew up on my walls. Then it would take them a while as they went around my apartment reading. Some of the guys I dated before would get weirded out or ask me to take them down. Some were so freaked out they didn't know if we should date. That was fine by me. I was secure in myself and my positivity. (Ladies, if a man gets freaked out about you being ambitious or posting friendly reminders about how you are going to kick ass and make an impact on this world, then he probably isn't the one for you. But don't worry, the right guy is out there!)

    One of the craziest things that I have ever done on a date, back when I was single, this guy took me to the mall to do dinner and a movie and before we got to the movie, I stopped at this store that had a bunch of fake awards that looked like Oscars. Now, I have always wanted to be like Lady Gaga and Mark Ronson and others that won the best original song for *Shallow* from the film, *A Star Is Born*. So, I took one of these Oscars and pretended to give my acceptance speech for Best Original Song. I'm sure he thought, *this chick is nuts!* But I didn't care! I found a way to better envision my dream! It was funny, too and I made him take my picture with it. Me, acting like a Miss America pageant winner crying. But I just liked being able to hold the award and although it wasn't the real thing, it brought my imagination and my ability to envision myself accepting such an award. That week I went back and bought the fake Oscar and would practice various acceptance speeches at home in the mirror!

Terri Savelle Foy is a major advocate of having a vision board. She's had one every year since 2012 and she's seen an amazing difference that it's made. She even wrote a book about it entitled, *Dream it. Pin it. Live it.* Terri gushes over all the great things that her vision board has helped her achieve. She says, "When you see your dreams come to pass, one after another, you're convinced in the power of having a clear vision and keeping it before your eyes to manifest your dreams."

Terri says, "We are trained to frame our past, you know, by displaying pictures of what we've already done and accomplished, but see, your vision board is just the opposite. You're literally framing your future before it ever happens, and this is the fun part." I love that she says, "We are trained to frame our past". That's so great. Perhaps, that's why we tend to live in our past and continue to recreate and manifest our past over and over. Maybe it's because we are looking at it all the time! You want to start looking where you are going! You want to start focusing on where you are headed! Not where you have been! The past is the past! And that's old news!

You want to surround yourself with pictures and images of your vision and put pressure on those dreams and visions to come alive. Maybe you want to travel to a foreign country, drive a certain type of car, or reach a new height in your business that you have never gone to before! Nothing is impossible if you have faith, work on yourself and strive to make your dreams a reality!

Before you make a vision board or start posting pictures and making your living space a scrapbook of what's to come, really think about what it is you want. Take time out of your day to sit quietly and list the things that you would like to see manifest, whether it be something like a certain amount of subscribers, a certain person you would like to meet, how much money you would like to make or a new home.

"Goals are simply dreams with deadlines." - Terri Savelle Foy

Think about things that you would like to accomplish over the next year in all aspects of your life and not just one. Imagine it being the end of the year and the countdown to the new year is happening and you find yourself looking back on the amazing year you had. The things that come to mind are what you need to be putting on your vision board and surrounding yourself with. Everyday I get up and get started. Run towards the accomplishment of these worthy goals.

What I am saying is your vision needs to be sound. You need to see it in your mind before you will ever see it manifest in your life. Lady Gaga said something that I can relate to myself (yes, this makes me sound extremely cocky and arrogant. Oh well, I don't care.) Kids cover your ears. She said, "I used to walk down the street like I was a fucking star... I want people to walk around delusional about how great they can be - and then to fight so hard for it every day that the lie becomes the truth." See that is what I mean by the title of this book. I want you to walk around like you have already accomplished your goals and dreams and when you do that you start to become that person. You are true to the definition of who you believe you are. Many people have told me to get my head out of the clouds, to take off my rose-colored glasses, or that I am delusional. Well, I hate to break it to you, but it's been working well for me so far! I love my life! Could it be better, yes! But who's life couldn't? My life is awesome, and I love living happy and what some would call "delusional!" It works for me! You can try it too! Doesn't cost you anything, either! Best thing ever, right? ☺

What Is It That You Want?

"You do not succeed because you do not know what you want, but because you don't want it intensely enough." -Frank Crane

Think about all areas of your life. What do you want to weigh? What do you want your bank account or salary to look like? What kind of home do you want? What kind of clothes do you want to wear? What kind of image do you want to project? What kind of relationships do you want to have; romantic, family, work, etc.? What kind of spiritual/religious practices do you want to put in place? How do you want to give back to your community? What kind of impact do you want to leave behind? What kind of business do you want to have or not have?

All these questions are important to answer. Take some time to think about these and begin to take small actions everyday towards becoming the person you want to be. Maybe that means making five sales calls a day. Maybe that means making a website for your cupcake business you are going to start in the kitchen of your own home. Whatever it is, don't just have goals in one area or certain areas of your life. The person you are to be is who you are now becoming.

You have to take a look at all the aspects of your life and mold yourself into the dream and vision that you have for yourself. Do you want to spend less time at your job so you can spend more time with your kids? Well, news flash, just wanting it doesn't make it happen and I will be the first to tell you about the power of our thoughts, but you must be taking action.

Consistency and accountability are two things that will really help you stay on target when it comes to going after your dreams. When I decided to run my first half marathon (so far, I have run two. But I can do better.) I told everyone and their brother that I was running the half marathon at the end of April. That way I would look like a complete and total ass if I dropped out or didn't run it. I also would have to tell them all what time I ran it in. And so, I didn't look like a slow ass turtle, I wanted to run it with a decent time.

I looked up half marathon training schedules online for people who weren't terribly out of shape and I found one I really liked. I wrote my training schedule down on every calendar I had (mind you, usually I have between 4 and 5). I would run farther on the weekends than through the week after work with one or two rest days a week. I was committed to this plan and I followed through. I remember crying when I crossed the finish line because I knew my father who had passed away when I was eleven who had always struggled with his weight would have been so, so proud of me.

Les Brown has a saying about commitment that I find humorous but at the same time wonderful imagery to describe what commitment means. Say you are eating breakfast and you have a plate of bacon and eggs. Les Brown says, "chicken was involved but the pig was committed" If you don't understand, he is saying the chicken just had to lay an egg, but the pig had to die so you could eat your morning bacon.

Tony Robbins, another one of my favorite speakers says, "If you want to take the island you need to burn the boats." This means no going back, no matter what. No plan b. No, maybe, maybe not. Be committed to becoming who you dreamed of being and living the life you intended on. You can have whatever it is you want. Get your mind and your actions in line and you will become unstoppable.

Lewis Gordon said, "There is nothing more powerful than the made-up mind." Make up your mind. And become a force to be reckoned with. People will be jealous of your dreams and of your positivity and jealous of the fact that you have something that propels you out of bed in the morning. Don't let them stop you. I like to think of the people who try to tear down my dreams like the dementors in J.K. Rowling's Harry Potter series. They just suck the life out of you because they are resentful, they gave up on their dreams and mad it didn't work out for them.

    Have faith that your dreams will come to pass and work on your dreams and yourself daily. Don't listen to anyone who tries to tell you differently.

Only Compare Yourself to Who You Were Yesterday

"Comparison is an act of violence against the self."
- Iyanla Vanzant.

    Clinical Psychologist Jordan B. Peterson has a chapter (or should I say it's one of his dozen rules) in his book *12 Rules for Life – An Antidote to Chaos.* This right here is SO important. We live very different lives today than the ones of our parents or even grandparents. With this being so, we must remember that people only show on social media what they want to show and what they want you to see. Stop comparing yourself to that woman that you THINK has the perfect marriage, you are not a fly on the wall of her home. You don't know what's REALLY going on behind closed doors. Stop comparing yourself to that person that just got a promotion and is farther ahead of you in their career. You don't know where they started, how hard they worked, what they may have sacrificed or what help they may have received. Stop comparing yourself to that woman who just had a baby that you have been trying so desperately to have. Perhaps, it's not your time. Your child may not be ready to manifest him or herself into this physical realm yet and join you. Wait and be patient. What you know is for you is for you and will happen in perfect divine time.

Another trouble with comparing yourself to someone else is that we are all human. Odds are that although that person may not show it, or you may not perceive them to have flaws. They do. We all do. And that doesn't make us bad. It simply makes us human. So, take whoever it is you have been wanting to be or take whatever it is that you have been wanting to possess down from its pedestal. What is meant for you, will be yours. You are exactly where and who you are meant to be at this exact date and time. Now, that doesn't mean that you can't strive to be more, to do more and to give more. But what it does mean is that you let yourself off the hook for not keeping up with everyone and everything. Except yourself for who you are and where you are at. All of what you are experiencing now is needed today to get you where you need to be tomorrow! Embrace it!

Never Compare Yourself! TO ANYONE! It does not do you any good. And you know what it does? IT WASTES YOUR TIME. Time you can't get back. Wealthy people are more upset when you steal their time from them than money. Time is something we can't get back. Once it's gone, it's gone. That's why quality is more important than quantity when spending time with your loved ones.

Never tell them (no matter how mad you are) "I just spent (X) hours with you! What more do you want from me?" News flash buddy, they want you present and in the moment. They want you to see and hear them for who they are! They want you to be a witness to their soul! They want to know that they matter, and they are enough! So, when you are spending time with your family and loved ones, put your phone away. Put your laptop and tablets down and just BE with them! They will appreciate that more than you know!

    My favorite line in the song *Three Wooden Crosses* sung by Randy Travis and written by Kim Williams and Doug Johnson is "I guess it's not what you take when you leave this world behind you. It's what you leave behind you when you go." There it is, in black and white people. It's not about the material stuff! It's not about you driving a Lamborghini or Jenny having the latest and greatest pair of red bottoms! It is about your impact and your legacy and how many people's lives you've touched in a positive way. How many people can you, have you and will you help! Who cares if you aren't a certain size or didn't take the quarterback to prom? What kind of person are you and what have you done for others? Focus on yourself! Go inward and examine what areas of you and your personality you may need to work on! Focus on what areas of your life where you are just rocking it out and ask yourself how you can get better at that? Ask yourself how you can be better than the person you were yesterday? Stop focusing on what the girl you don't like at work is doing or what your neighbor down the street just did to update their home! This is about you and you serving others!

In an article by Susan Biali Haas, M.D. in Psychology Today has a couple of tips that may help you, so you aren't always falling prey to comparison. They are as follows:

1. Become aware of, and avoid, your triggers.
2. Remind yourself that other people's "outsides" can't be compared to your "insides"
3. Repeat whenever necessary: "Money doesn't buy happiness, and never will"
4. Be grateful for the good in your life, and resist any lies that shout "It's not enough"

I think all these are super important when you find yourself feeling envious, lonely, sad or depressed after scrolling through social media and letting someone else's financial success or relational success get to you. Just remember, people only put what they want you to see on social media and there is more to all of us than meets the eye. Don't be envious of anyone when you don't even know the whole story.

Keep in mind that you are enough, just as you are and money can only buy you happiness temporarily. A new dress or pair of shoes for us women makes us feel so wonderful. But that feeling is only temporary. True happiness regardless of conditions is much more important.

Just focus on being better than you were yesterday. Bob Proctor says, "Better is beautiful." Whether it is being a better parent, spouse, colleague, friend, or mentor, focusing on being better will enhance your performance and strengthen your relationships. Maybe your better is hitting a sales goal that you have never reached before or earning substantially more this year than you did last year. Whatever it is, focus on improving. Look for books, seminars, online classes, retreats, mentors, audiobooks, groups you can join, networking events, etc. Most people want to share the knowledge that they have learned and are willing to help you if you ask. Especially since we have the internet there is no reason why you can't take your life and become the highest, truest expression of yourself.

Build Your House on Solid Rock, Leave the Sand Alone

"When the ego weeps for what it has lost, the spirit rejoices for what it has found." -Eckhart Tolle paraphrasing an ancient Sufi saying

One day, during the time of quarantine that was advised due to the coronavirus' impact on the US, I woke up and was not my normal happy and motivated self. It had been raining for what seemed like weeks on end, we were being told to stay home and not go out except for the essentials, the economy was rapidly falling, and I had a person in my family battling a very real sickness. I just was not my normal, positive, grateful and happy self. That day, while on YouTube, I stumbled upon a video with Eckhart Tolle and he referenced the bible and talked about the scripture where it talks about building your house on a solid foundation and not that of sand. And I always knew the importance of this because my stepfather is in excavating. So, I know all about the importance of a solid foundation. But this day it hit me differently.

Eckhart was talking about the metaphor of the house being you and your spiritual, emotional, and mental foundation needs to be firm and solid. I don't know why I had never thought about that phrase in that way before. I had always taken the metaphor to be referring to either your literal house or your relationship with your significant other. That I understood. But this new way of looking at it was something I had never considered before.

While on my morning walk, I began to realize I had been thinking about stabilizing my house, my relationship and ideas for future businesses on a solid foundation but I had not thought about myself. Don't be so focused on external things that you forget to do the internal work. That is so important.

When you face difficult times, think about what they can teach you. What can you learn from this? Storms help you grow. Tolle basically says that you won't grow in your comfort zone. This storm was made to thrust you out of your comfort zone and catapult you into the next level. It's meant to shape you and prepare you for what you will face in the future. If nothing ever went wrong in your life you would not have the growth you have.

"People only evolve through the challenges they encounter." Eckhart Tolle

Use the problems you face to become better and learn and put things into place so you will be better prepared for when the storm hits. Don't just sit around and complain, 'Woe is me." People really don't want to hear it and unfortunately, in our society not too many people care. Other people are fighting their own dragons and battling their own storms. How selfish would you be to think that you are the only one! You got this! This is meant to teach you and better you! Not hold you back!

"In a good movie, the protagonist or the character changes as he or she faces the problem or what goes wrong in the movie." –Eckhart Tolle

Be like a good movie, take the good and bad of life and be able to WITHSTAND it. Use every difficulty you face to better you and make you stronger. Be sure to build on a solid foundation, even if that means that you must tear down and rebuild.

When we think of the world's most amazing beaches and islands we think of places like Bora Bora, Bali, The Philippines, the impressive resorts and islands in The Caribbean. These are places that we fly to on vacation and stay for a week. We go snorkeling, hiking, biking and lay by the pool. We get massages, drink too much and get sunburnt.

What we don't realize about the fantastic houses on the water and beach houses that we book for our vacations, is that one storm could wipe it all away.

Think about this when it comes to your marriage, future marriage and friendships. Who is it that you are spending your time with and how strong are your mental, emotional, and perhaps, physical bonds? What will your relationship be able to withstand when the storms come or is your relationship with that person, merely a surface level relationship built on the sand.

Think of building your business on solid rock. Depression and recession are going to strike. What will you have in place to make sure your business isn't taken out by the hurricane? What will you be able to contribute with the time comes? What new ideas will your company present to the market to improve the quality of other people's lives?

I think of the tornadoes that hit Nashville, Hermitage and Mt. Juliet in March 2020. A lot of people lost or had damage done to their homes and some people even lost their lives. Some people's roofs were ripped right off, but their houses were made of brick and remained mostly if not all the way intact. What are you made up of? Have you taken the time to work on your personal development? Have you taken the time to work on your problems instead of masking them with appearances or hiding them with substances?

Brick by brick you want to build your company. Brick by brick you want to build your relationships. Brick by brick you want to work on yourself. We are so caught up in society's false beliefs nowadays. Everyone thinks that they can get rich quick or take a pill and drop 50 pounds. I challenge you to take the hard way. Try doing things the right way and going the extra mile and putting in the extra effort. Do things right the first time.

A lot of people who are said to be an "overnight success" worked hard for at least 15 years or more to do what they do. So, don't think they had it easy or be envious of them because you think they had this or that! They paved their road to success by laying brick by brick while you are over here with a dump truck pouring cement and taking the easy route. Remember, build quality relationships, build a quality business, work on becoming a person of quality and you will be able to withstand the storms, when they do in fact come.

Negative Thoughts Are a Rabbit Hole

"Negative thinking definitely attracts negative results." -Norman Vincent Peale

Jim Rohn said, "Everyday stand guard at the door of your mind." This is so important.

Joyce Meyer has a book called, *The Battlefield of the Mind.*

Psychologists will tell you that 70% or more of our thoughts are negative. That to me is shocking. Because when we entered this world as children, we were confident and proud and lacked the insecurities that most of us have today. Those insecurities were learned and taught to us. Our creator, I believe (whichever name you prefer to use), created us with only love and confidence in ourselves and others. Children have a blind belief and enthusiasm which is remarkable.

If you cannot win the war that is going on in your own mind day in and day out, you more than likely will not succeed in your own life. You have to march in with your sword every time a negative thought begins to creep up. If you don't squash it right away, that thought will grow and lead to more and exponentially lead to more negative thoughts and those thoughts will begin to manifest in your own life. That is the danger of not being in control of your own mind. Everyone knows this and can attest to it but not many put forward the effort that it requires.

Dr. Bruce Lipton says that negative thinking is called, The Nocebo Effect. It has just as powerful an effect on our biology as positive thinking does. And knowing this, why would you not do all that you could to think in such a way that benefits your overall health?

One day I was watching Dr. Oz and Tony Robbins was there and he was speaking to four women about how to create the change in their lives that they desired. Tony asked the women about what someone who suffers from depression or is depressed looks like and they talked about the following; poor posture, rounded shoulders, quiet voice, slow movements, etc. And he spoke to the women about how in order to get different results one thing that they needed to do was to change their state. For instance, throw your shoulders back, speak quickly, loudly and confidently, move with intention, smile, keep your head up, don't have your head down and look at the floor, look people in the eye when you are speaking to them, etc. These are all things that you can do that will help if you are in a negative state that will provide you with small immediate results.

"No one knows enough to be a pessimist about anything." -Dr. Wayne Dyer

Another thing that you can do to combat negativity in your life is to turn off the news! And if for some odd reason you cannot do that I highly encourage you to drastically reduce the amount of news you consume. Yes, you need to know what's going on. You need to be informed of candidates and their policies when you go to vote. You need to know about storms, when and if they are coming and the necessary actions you need to take to keep you and your family safe. But a news overload will depress you and make you feel as if the world is a worse place than what it is!

I would also encourage you to limit or eliminate the time you spend watching violent or gory movies and television shows. The same goes with video games. Fill your world with positivity. Perhaps, you could spend that extra hour a day watching the news and turn it into a cooking channel and learn to make some new dishes for you and your family! Or perhaps you could turn it to the history channel and learn some cool facts about the history of the human race that you didn't know! Or maybe try to turn it to National Geographic and learn about different animal species and geographic regions!

Take your routine and look at the areas that are weak and where you have gaps. Instead of listening to rap on your way to work, that makes you feel like life has handed you the short end of this stick, try listening to an audio book, a motivational speech, a classical piece of music, gospel, or happy jazz (as I like to call it.) Your reality is what you perceive it to be. That's a wonderful secret that not too many of us know. You can choose to believe that most people are good and are willing to aid you on your journey or you can think that all you have is a giant black cloud following you with bad luck. The choice is yours and the effort is somewhat the same.

Surround yourself with audio, visuals, textures, and smells that delight you, make you feel happy and aligned with source. If something puts you at ease and quiets your mind! If something makes you feel invincible and empowered, embrace that, too! Get rid of these things in your life that make you feel inadequate, depressed, angry, or like you are living in fear. Fear and negative thoughts can control you and run your life.

Know that Napoleon Hill said, "Whatever the mind can conceive and believe, the mind can achieve." This works both ways. So, why not use it for its highest good?

Romans 12:2 King James Version (KJV)

2 And be not conformed to this world: but be ye transformed by the renewing of your mind,

that ye may prove what is that good, and acceptable, and perfect, will of God.

A lot of people don't achieve their hopes, goals, and dreams because they suffer from stinkin' thinkin'. They think the same as the next person. Be transformed and constantly work on your mind. Be aware of the thoughts and words that you are accepting and letting influence you. The work you do on your mind is like the journey of mastery. There is always something to learn. You can find better ways of executing your daily tasks and you can find ways of looking at things that you never thought of before!

Positive Thinking

"How to be positive- Say 'I can,' instead of 'I can't!' Smile more. Be optimistic. Remember you are in charge. Be thankful. Forget about regret. Do nice things for others." — Unknown

An article by the very well mind cites that "The Mayo Clinic reports a number of health benefits associated with optimism, including a reduced risk of death from cardiovascular problems, less depression and an increased lifespan." Researchers are not entirely certain on why positive thinking and optimism is so good for you. They assume it's linked to healthier habits that promote a healthier lifestyle than your average Joe. But no matter what the reason is for these results the results are real! It is so important to see the glass half full instead of it half empty!

Positive thinking is also believed to play a major role in resilience and overcoming hardship! Instead of focusing on the problem, positive people focus on the solution and the benefits of having the overall experience! Positive people have been found to be more resourceful and more willing to ask for help when they need it, which probably lightens their load! Positive thinking can help you manage stress better and develop better coping skills when problems arise!

I think it's important to acknowledge that positive thinking doesn't mean that you ignore the challenges that life presents. It just means that you approach solving them with more positivity and in an overall more productive manner. When you are presented with a problem you should get excited that you are now on a mission to provide an answer, provide a solution. Without the problem you may not have ever come to that conclusion. Just remember that you can't always control what happens to you, but you can control how you react to the situation! A lot of times our issues are opportunities undercover!

In an article on mayoclinic.org called *Positive thinking: Stop negative self-talk to reduce stress,* they listed the health benefits of having a positive outlook on life. They are as follows:

- Increased life span
- Lower rates of depression
- Lower levels of distress
- Greater resistance to the common cold
- Better psychological and physical well-being
- Better cardiovascular health and reduced risk of death from cardiovascular disease
- Better coping skills during hardships and times of stress

If knowing this alone doesn't change your mind to switch to looking on the bright side, I'm shocked. When I learned this, I was impressed that positive thinking can do all that, but I wasn't surprised. Your life really does improve if you just keep on the sunny side!

Dr. Bruce Lipton has found that changing the way you perceive the world changes your overall biology, which in turn changes your cells. So, if you can control your mind you are capable of endless possibilities. Keep in mind, however, there are two parts to the mind, the conscious and the subconscious. That's why the section of this book entitled *Rewriting Negative Programming* is so important. You can't only program the conscious mind and expect to live a positive life. You must also reprogram the subconscious mind, as well.

Finding opportunities to laugh and smile is a great way to become more positive. Whether that means listening to a humorous podcast while driving around town or laughing at yourself when you do something embarrassing like fall, trip, or something of that nature, a little bit goes a long way. Find things that make you smile and make you laugh and make them a part of your everyday life.

I really love comedians. But sometimes I find that they are a little too crude for my taste. That is why I love people like Ellen DeGeneres. I read her book, *Seriously I'm Kidding* in less than three days while I was in college and my roommates always wondered why I was upstairs cracking up, by myself. I like her standup and her show too. I love her sense of humor because normally it isn't offensive and it's not crude like some other comedians. I love Ellen. Ellen, if you're reading this, can we be friends?

    One thing that I touch on later in the book is the old saying that birds of a feather flock together. It's true when you are talking about positivity, as well. You cannot surround yourself with negative people and expect to live a positive life! Again, let me repeat, YOU CANNOT SURROUND YOURSELF WITH NEGATIVE PEOPLE AND EXPECT TO LIVE A POSITIVE LIFE! Be mindful of people's energy when they approach you and are around you. If someone exudes negative energy, I think that it's best that you slowly start distancing yourself from that person. On the contrary, if you are around someone and they make you feel like all you need is your superhero cape and you can save the world, try spending more time with that person! It's so important to surround yourself with people who make you feel good and people who inspire you! If you feel emotionally drained, that's a sign that you need to start running in a different circle and you may need to schedule more alone time with yourself, too!

    Getting outside and getting fresh air (especially, if you live in a city. Trust me.) and some sunlight will do wonders and lift your mood! I guarantee it! Get active! Go for a walk, hike, bike, or run. Get your friend or lover to go on a picnic in the park with you! Go play frisbee with your dog or teach your dog agility at a dog park! You will feel like a total badass for teaching your dog to do something you didn't know he could, and your dog will be happy to please his owner!

Maybe your boost of endorphins could come from going to a gym and lifting weights, getting on the stair stepper or rowing machine! Perhaps, you need to go to the Y and do some laps in the pool. Maybe you're the kind of person that loves early morning yoga! Whatever it is, find what works for you and get active! Try to stay physically active and try to spend time outside doing things that stimulate your body and mind. It will make you smile, feel more youthful and stand a little taller!

Take some time when you are upset and do deep breathing. Go for a walk or do something to relieve stress in a productive and healthy manner if you can. Then come back and revisit what upsets you if you can. Perhaps, your initial reaction to the situation was out of proportion or perhaps, it was just right. You want to make sure you can become calm before doing or saying something you regret. Positive people aren't flying off the handle every chance they get. Most of the time, they handle even the biggest challenges with grace, maturity, and courage!

Another thing that I touch on in another section of the book that I will touch on now, as well (because it really is that important) is positive self-talk. Be mindful of how you talk to yourself in your head or out loud. Don't let negativity (which is only there to prevent you from reaching your full potential) get you down! Encourage yourself and be your own best friend! Be the cheerleader that you never had! Tell yourself that you can do anything you set your mind to and work hard at. Because, guess what, YOU CAN! You are the only person standing in the way of your own goals, dreams, and desires! Be delusional! Convince yourself that you can do, be or have anything! You can! Shoot for the moon! Nothing is off limits! Tell yourself that you have a great memory! Tell yourself that you are beautiful, charming and smart! Tell yourself people love you, want to be friends with you and want to do business with you! Tell yourself things are working out in your favor! And put a halt on all that negativity!

God's thoughts are not your thoughts. God or the universe can dream bigger, much bigger than you. And source may have a different journey in mind for you than the journey you thought was meant for you. Life has a funny way of surprising us, so dress up, show up and never give up!

Life is very cyclical. So, if you are going through a tough time right now, just hang in there because the storms don't last forever. It may seem like no one understands you or that you are all alone but just remember that there are no new problems. Everything that you have ever faced or will face, someone has experienced that before. Look for answers and guidance from people who are smarter than you and have experience in dealing with what you are dealing with.

Your perception determines your reality. You can think of a problem or issue as the end of the road or you can think of it as a hurdle that a track runner (you are the track runner in this case) has to jump over in order to out run the opponents and take the prized medal. Just remember if you are not willing to grow and learn and become a better person because of having to get over that hurdle, there are 10 other people behind you who are.

Look in the mirror and tell yourself every morning, noon, and night, that you love yourself! As the old African Proverb says, "If there is no enemy within, then the enemy outside can do us no harm." Some of you may be thinking, *'I don't even know what that means!'* While others may be thinking, *'I know exactly what that means but here she comes with the definition…'* Hell right, I am! What it means is if you have no inner battles going on and you are at peace, happy and content with yourself nothing can touch you! Now, is that easier said than done. OF COURSE, IT IS! Doesn't mean that we can't all try to get there!

By looking in the mirror daily and telling yourself that you love who you are, it sets you on the right path to becoming who you are meant to be and fulfilling your goals/dreams. When you don't love who you are you will shrink into a shell and believe that you are undeserving or less worthy than what you truly are! Remember we are all a part of the divine and a part of source. We are God and God is us!

Part of my problem in achieving success musically, was that when I got around talented male musicians that I didn't believe that I was good enough. I would start singing a song that I had sung a million times and due to fears of not being good enough I would burst into tears and not be able to finish the rest of the song, lesson, and/or set. This took me years to get over. I had to think about myself as worthy to be on the stage with those talented male musicians. Even if I didn't know as much as they knew. I still had gifts and talents to offer that are unique and as valuable as theirs. So, it's a mix.

You really must find the balance between feeling confident and deserving but not being overbearing and cocky and thinking that you are better than others. You need to keep a sense of humbleness about you at the same time. And this took me a long time to figure out. At times, it still trips me up. So, think positively!

Have an Open Mind

"Have a mind that's open to everything and attached to nothing." – Dr. Wayne Dyer

He says, "That's an interesting point of view. I've never considered that." Perhaps, new thoughts are not new thoughts. Perhaps, they are just old thoughts regenerated. And I think it's crucial for growth and evolution to be open to plenty of things. It doesn't mean that you must compromise who you are or your morals. It just means that it is essential not to be close-minded and shut off from the world.

"Progress is impossible if you do things the way you've always done." – Dr. Wayne Dyer

People who have an open mind don't lack a belief system or aren't followers or lost people. Open-minded people are just unafraid to say something like, "I've never thought of it that way."

Having an open mind allows you to build on the foundation you already have and become more of who you are. An open mind will open you up to new possibilities and experiences. It is essential to know that despite what we may think, we don't know everything. We know very little. There is so much room for growth and study.

"The fool doth think he is wise, but the wise man knows himself to be a fool." -William Shakespeare, As You Like It

That is exactly what he is saying here. A wise person knows that they know not. Once you think you have got life all figured out, I promise you that life will shock and surprise you. You are never done learning, growing, evolving, and becoming your highest self.

I found this quote when I was going about my business yesterday (not even try to research or find the subject matter to support topics in my book). It blew me away.

"You are to your own life like a great painter is to his or her own creation." -Dr. Wayne Dyer

I love that. Just picture yourself in a constant state of becoming and in pursuit of mastery, like an artist masters the paints and the canvas and a saxophone player masters his instrument. You are too foolish to know everything and too foolish to have already been exposed to everything needed to help you grow.

Being an open-minded person helps you grow and not to become closed off to the world, ideas, or the wants/needs of others. It gives you the confidence needed to be that perpetual student and admit that there are things you would like to learn and that there still is a lot that you do not know. It takes a very confident and secure person to admit this. And I know what you are thinking, *it takes confidence to admit you don't know certain things? Come on, Anna, I thought you were going to tell me something riveting. Why did I even buy this book?*

Think about older adults who take college classes to get a second degree or perhaps, their first or maybe even to gain the GED they never received. That takes immense courage and an open mind. It takes someone who has the strength of character to go back to school. It takes confidence to sit there in class among people who are much younger than you. These people are humble and admit that they do not know it all.

Honesty is also often a characteristic of people with an open mind. It takes honesty to admit downfalls, weaknesses, and areas that could be improved or see things from someone else's perspective. Open-minded people are often people, as well, who will admit their mistakes, own up to them, and be able to empathize. They are open to the possibility that they played a part in their current situation. Not just the possibility but the fact that they did. Often, you are where you are because of you and no one else. Look for spiritual teachers, counselors, mentors, and other people that can help you if you are not where you would like to be. When you try to reach out, most people will go out of their way to help!

Brene Brown talks a great deal about vulnerability. How scary yet freeing it is both at the same time. Open-minded people share this dichotomy of fearfulness and the sense of being free. They excuse themselves by allowing themselves to be vulnerable enough to know that they can always learn from the person in front of them or the problem presented to them. You will be amazed at what life has to offer you when you take down the walls of rigidity.

Now, I'm not saying that you must, but you may change if you choose to start having an open mind. You may find your beliefs changing, the foods you like, the music you listen to, the people you hang out with, and the place(s) that you live in. Be open to the possibility that this may happen. Some people are open-minded but still have the same beliefs. Some people become open minded and start to shift. You don't have to believe the same, dress the same, talk, walk or behave the same as everyone in your family or anyone else that you grew up with. You have the right to acknowledge what does and doesn't work for you and act on it. Do what makes you happy. Look at life with fresh eyes and don't fall prey to the peer pressures of society.

One of the hardest things about having an open mind is releasing the ability/want to control people, things, and situations. Having an open mind means that things may not always work out the way you planned, and you can see other alternatives and you are okay with the alternatives you can't see. It also means that beliefs held by you and/or others might be challenged. Just because someone looks at something differently than you doesn't make them necessarily wrong. It means that they disagree or see things differently. Some of the most outstanding debaters were the ones that could empathize with their opponents' point of view. Therefore, they could predict what they might say next, examine the holes in their argument, and bring them to light.

Allow your mind to be freed from limiting beliefs. Allow yourself to look at solutions to your problems differently. Allow yourself to have more fun in life, take more chances and try things that you never thought you would. Allow yourself to be less judgmental and see and accept people as they are. Understanding that your way of living may not be the necessary "right" way to live (I tell you as I write this book). Allow yourself to become more patient and understanding, realizing that the world does not revolve around you and that there might be an excellent reason that someone is acting the way they are. Do not be afraid to ask questions, face rejection, or learn something new.

The opposite of being open-minded is closed-minded. Most close-minded people are not open or receptive to new ideas, changes, or thoughts. Without open-mindedness, we slow the progression of humankind. Innovation and radical changes within technologies, communication, dress, and other aspects of life were all put in place by open-minded people. Ideas and adaptation are essential to invention. We'd risk stagnation if all of us were closed-minded. Overall, I believe we need a certain balance of closed- and open-minded individuals. All I know is that I have benefited a great deal from being open-minded myself.

Taking Classes

"Continuous learning is the minimum requirement for success in any field." -Brian Tracy

When my mom was growing up, my grandpa worked for Ford, and despite a bit of work here and there, my grandma stayed home. We live in different times now. You can't just have a career job and never learn anything more or train yourself to become more skilled.

The world is constantly changing and evolving. Tony Robbins always says, "Happiness equals progress." So, you know what that means…? You are too! Changing and evolving and becoming someone new!

Your body regenerates with all new cells every 7 to 10 years! Can you believe that? Isn't that nuts? So, why aren't you working with it? Why aren't you working on becoming a new and better version of yourself constantly? Taking classes can help you do this.

Whether you want to be a famous jazz singer and want to hone your skills by getting into some theory, vocal tech classes and jazz ensembles or if you want to become rich and so you enroll in Dave Ramsey's Financial Peace University, there are always classes that you can find that will help guide you in achieving even your most lofty of goals. And don't even tell me that you don't know where to look. Nowadays, with the internet, everything is at our fingertips. There is no excuse for you not to learn!

"I don't have the money to take classes." Yeah, I've heard that one too. Skillshare is a great affordable way to take classes for only $15.00 a month. And don't say you can't afford $15.00 a month. You spend that on Starbucks coffee, wine, or beer.

Jack Canfield and Tony Robbins have great online seminars, workshops, weekend retreats, and events for anyone interested in checking out. Jack says, "You have to learn more to earn more." And I agree. If you don't, other people will, at any age, which can be dangerous to your success if you are not learning all the time.

Suppose you are not ready to expand your horizons and take classes to better yourself in this modern age. Someone else will take advantage of what is being offered and eventually take your place. They will surpass you simply because you were lazy and made excuses.

Some people decide to take classes simply for mental stimulation and social interaction. Taking classes is a great way to meet people and make connections, all while learning new things and improving the person you are! Perhaps, you are terrified of public speaking. Why not push yourself outside of your comfort zone and build your self-confidence by mastering something that you didn't even know you had it in you to do? Perhaps, you always wanted to learn how to cook because you are an inner-city chick and your main dish (that everyone knows you by) is Chinese takeout. There are plenty of cooking classes you can take, online and in person. You could get a culinary degree. Or you could subscribe to a cooking channel on YouTube and try to duplicate the recipes/meals. Perhaps, your dream is to get into real estate and start selling houses as a side hustle until you make enough money to leave your current job. Well, take those classes and study and pass that exam and get your license!

If you are someone who likes to travel perhaps, taking classes to learn a new language is right for you. Imagine visiting Japan and being able to carry on a conversation with the locals in their language! Imagine just how awesome that would be! You could make a new friend instead of just being another tourist asking for directions!

Tony Robbins says that "Progress equals happiness." And he is so right. When you feel as if you are growing and improving day in and day out, you feel happy, and when you're not growing, you'll find you aren't that happy. I think that this is one of the benefits of taking classes and educating yourself, you boost your level of happiness when you do this.

Plus, just think of all the positive side effects of taking classes. You can earn more money, meet new people and grow as a person. You more than likely will be able to create a better quality of life for you and your family.

As an adult learner you have your experience behind you and maturity, and you are more focused than most people in college courses. This gives you an advantage to fully absorb the material being presented and not have the distractions of your youth. Taking classes is a great way to expand your horizons and broaden your mind. If you think that learning has stopped or will stop when you get your degree, think again. The best at what they do, never stop learning!

Give to Others

"The secret to living is giving." – Tony Robbins

In an article on greatergood.berkley.edu called *5 Ways Giving Is Good for You* by Jason Marsh and Jill Suttie they state that giving money to others makes us happier than if we spend the money on ourselves. Giving to charities is stated to activate parts of our brain and give us a glow. The giving provides us with social connection, trust, and pleasure. We feel good that we did something other than for ourselves.

In people with chronic illness giving has been proven to improve health. People who volunteer once to twice a week are 44 percent less likely to die within five years than non-volunteers, according to a 1999 out of the University of California, Berkeley, led by Doug Oman. This statistic shocked me; I'll admit. But it just goes to show the true power of giving back to our communities and others. We are meant to improve the lives of one another and give what we can, when we can.

Giving, like several other topics mentioned in this book, has also been proven to lower stress and blood pressure. Keep in mind, however, that it is important for us to only pour from a cup that's full. There is a quote that says, "You can't give away what you don't have." You can't give away anything: money, love, joy, happiness, etc. if you don't first have it to give. Too many times people make this mistake. I am not asking you to pour from an empty cup or donate money when you are wondering how to pay your bills. But what I am calling for, is that you make giving a priority in your life and that you give in whatever way that you can. It is so important.

A lot of people will tell you to tithe 10 percent of your income to your church or place of worship, and why I don't think that isn't good sound advice, I don't think that you should put limits on WHERE or TO WHOM you give. My best piece of advice is to give to places and people who touch your heart.

I give to the Nashville Jazz Workshop, donate money to help feed a child in a country that isn't as well off as we are, and I donate to St. Jude's Children's Hospital. I also will donate time or supplies to the Nashville Rescue mission and try to lend a helping hand to the Bridge Ministries, directed by Candy Christmas. I am not telling you this to brag. I'm telling you this because when I do these things, I feel better about myself and I feel happier.

I know churches do a lot, especially around the holidays, to help people in third world countries and put food on the tables of families who can't afford it. Whether you are donating $5.00 or $50,000.00, know that no amount is too small, and no amount is too much. And don't let anyone make you feel bad for trying to do a good deed. People will try to cut you down at times for trying to give and help and I know it sounds strange, like *why would someone do that?* But people will try. They will say your charity is corrupt or that you're too much of a goodie goodie. Don't let them get you down. Give unselfishly. Give and do not look for the approval of others. Give because it is the right thing to do and it makes you feel good.

When you give it strengthens the bonds between people and promotes social interaction, connection and cooperation. When people ban together simply to improve the lives of others, sometimes strangers that they don't even know, wonderful things happen. Most of the time you can feel it in the air.

Giving to others reminds us to be grateful for what we have and all the things day in and day out that we take for granted. (Gratitude has its own section in this book, too.) It also perpetuates more giving. When someone is kind and generous to you, often that puts you in the mindset of abundance and not the mindset of fear and lack. Because of this we tend to give more to others and become more empathetic and kinder ourselves. Giving, all around is a win-win. You can't go wrong. I was once told that giving to others and volunteering added more happiness to our lives than a $5,000.00 raise and I agree with that.

An article on time.com called *The Secret to Happiness is Helping Others* by Jenny Santi starts off with an old Chinese saying which reads, "If you want happiness for an hour, take a nap. If you want happiness for a day, go fishing. If you want happiness for a year, inherit a fortune. If you want happiness for a lifetime, help somebody." It's funny how decades and centuries and thousands of years can go by but there are still some fundamental things regarding humanity that remain the same. I don't know if our humanness will ever change.

Many times, people will call their profession or hobbies, their passion. Normally people can experience success in these areas because what our talents and abilities allow us to do is better serve others.

Conehealth.com states, "Giving has been proven to decrease blood pressure and reduce stress. This reduction promotes longer life and better health. Giving promotes social connection. Studies show that when you give to others, your generosity is often continued down the line to someone else or returned to you."

Never be afraid to give because when you do, it comes back to you tenfold. Giving is powerful and affects the giver almost as much, if not more than the receiver.

Rush.edu says that giving boosts your self-esteem and overall satisfaction in life. But that's not the only health benefit, it also puts you in better physical health and lowers your risk of depression. If you don't believe me, just check the facts!

Rush.edu also says, "Depression and lack of self-esteem have both been linked with heart disease and other health conditions. This link may partially explain why volunteering can lead to both better mental health and better physical health."

I found this very interesting physical health improves after volunteering or engaging in a generous act, that helps someone other than ourselves! The article also said, "Research on middle-aged and older adults, for example, has had similar findings. Middle-aged volunteers appear to have less belly fat, better cholesterol levels and lower blood sugar, compared with non-volunteers. And older adults who volunteer are less likely to have high blood pressure. This means, in turn, that they have lower risk for heart disease and stroke."

I don't know about you, but I am sure one of those people who would like to have less belly fat when I am middle aged, overall better health too.

People who have a purpose, a mission to serve others and/or act to alleviate suffering, not only have better physical health but better psychological health too. And they enjoy much longer lives as a result of both. Learning this, you might want to say to yourself, *what can I do for my community, my country, my world? How can I make a difference? How can I leave this world a little better than when I came?*

Although it's good to give, keep in mind that you can only give away what you have. Make sure your cup is full and your needs are being met. Balance is key in every aspect of life but do what you can, for as long as you can, as much as you can without wearing yourself out. Giving is what makes the world go 'round folks. And despite our negative media, it is happening all the time and everywhere!

Maslow's Hierarchy of Needs

"What is necessary to change a person is to change his awareness of himself." -Abraham Maslow

I encourage everyone who reads this book (if you haven't yet) to examine and learn about Maslow's Hierarchy of Needs. That may answer some questions for you. It might answer the question of why you feel stuck. Or maybe where other people you may know are in the hierarchy and maybe why they feel stuck. Please take some time and examine where you're at and write down some action steps to get to the next level. Keep in mind that this can take a lifetime. Do not become impatient if you don't shoot off like a rocket to the top of the hierarchy.

The first four levels of the pyramid can be described as "deficiency needs", and the top level is described as a "growth need." The motivation to fulfill the deficiency needs grows stronger and stronger the longer they go being unaccomplished. Once we meet one set of deficiency needs, our need to fulfill that in our mind will go away, and our new focus will be on the next level. However, that is not the case for the "growth" need of self-actualization. As you fulfill this need, you desire to continue to do more and more work in this area. You are motivated to continue and fly to higher heights.

In an article by simplypyschology.org on Maslow's Hierarchy of Needs, it is stated that "Growth needs do not stem from a lack of something, but rather from a desire to grow as a person." And I do think that this is the kick that Oprah is on. All joking aside, I think she is an excellent example to people of all ages.

Once these growth needs have been met, one can reach the highest level, which is self-actualization. Every soul on the planet earth desires to move up this hierarchy. This is a way to measure your journey to becoming your highest self. I think if people start focusing more on themselves and their personal growth, we would have a better world.

Life, however, throws us curveballs. So, the progression of this hierarchy is not always linear. We can encounter setbacks and surprises that we didn't see coming that makes us fluctuate between levels. Unfortunately, not everyone reaches self-actualization, but that doesn't mean you shouldn't be aiming for it.

I think it's important to always have a target and something you're always aiming at. When I am on my runs and walks, if I don't start an overall goal, I try to set milestones to focus on while on my run. Whether that be sprinting to the nearest stop sign or what have you. I believe that my performance as an athlete is heightened during this time as I narrow in on my goal. Nothing else exists, and I am laser-focused.

I used to tell my ex's three-year-old son to 'focus' and whatever he was doing at that time would improve, whether that meant getting off the john quicker or eating the food we decided was enough for him to eat to get down from the table. Once you narrow in your focus on becoming the truest, highest expression of yourself you won't have the time or energy to try to monitor and obsess over where anyone else is at in the race. You won't be criticizing your co-workers or boss, or neighbors as much. Instead, you will be spending more time thinking about you, how you can improve, and what your next step will be!

The first level of the pyramid is physiological needs. And this level is pretty basic and self-explanatory. They are basic survival needs: food, water, shelter, air, safety, warmth, sex, clothing, sleep, all the necessities. And I know some people take this level for granted, but even now, as I write this book, there are plenty of malnourished people who do not know where their next meal is coming from. So, please don't take these things for granted, and secondly, if you have the means, please donate money, time, or food so we can all meet this basic need. We have enough resources on the earth that no one should ever have to go hungry.

The second level is Safety needs. We all have a desire to feel safe and secure, whether we admit it or not. We have a need for feeling in control of our lives, in some way, shape, or form. We need to feel physically safe, emotionally safe, financially safe, mentally safe, and so on. There are different methods by which we try to achieve this type of safety. Whether that be through family, money stocked in the bank, armed forces, healthcare, the police, unemployment benefits, businesses, you name it. Most people can't have open and honest relationships if they don't feel safe, and a lot of creative ideas and entrepreneurship wouldn't have taken place had it not been for that person having a feeling of safety. When we feel safe, only then we allow ourselves to feel vulnerable. And I believe ideas and relationships need that safety and vulnerability to happen. Because most humans worry if they are good enough, and if that safety isn't there, they probably would never try. Some would. A lot of us would not.

The third level is called love and belonging needs. That means a need for social acceptance of some kind and to become part of a group such as a family, workgroup, friend group, etc. We need to feel loved and like we belong somewhere. Like wolves, we run in packs, and we all have this basic desire to find a pack that we belong to.

The fourth level is Esteem needs. First, the esteem needs are for us and then for others. When talking about the esteem needs for others, this might include reputation, respect, and status. For ourselves, it may be independence or a certain level of mastery or something of the like. People are very familiar with these needs even if they have never seen Maslow's hierarchy fully broken down. These needs are engrained and us. And like I said before, once we meet a set of deficiency needs, we develop an intense desire to fulfill the next level of desires almost immediately. We can see that taking place within ourselves and the lives of our friends, family, colleagues, and neighbors.

The top or fifth level is Self-actualization needs. That is the level that everyone strives for, but few achieve. Maslow in 1943 described this level as, "the desire to accomplish everything that one can, to become the most that one can be." That is what I am talking about, people! The highest, truest expression of one's self! That is when someone has reached self-fulfillment and living the best life that they possibly can! Not everyone achieves this level in the same way as the next. Some people want to be all they can be for their family, others want to leave their mark as an artist, some want to be a tremendous financial success and give millions away, and so on. That fact alone was an interesting one for me to learn. I never dreamed that there would be so many ways of becoming self-actualized. I think it's excellent! It is unique to the individual.

In 1987, Maslow stated that the structure of his hierarchy "is not nearly as rigid." Like I said before, some people fluctuate between levels, and for different individuals for different reasons, the order isn't always the same. Some people need self-esteem for love, and some starving artists sacrifice their basic needs for expressing their creative talents. His work is truly remarkable and exciting. It helps me define people's motivations, my motivations, and the characters in movies and books.

Also, in 1987 Maslow pointed out that when people do things, often there is just not only a set of needs behind it. Sometimes it can be all or any of the needs listed on his hierarchy.

Maslow's Motivation Model expands the growth needs into four areas: Cognitive needs, Aesthetic needs, Self-actualization, and Transcendence. Maslow was one of the few (like I talk about in this book) that in 1943, focused on the good in people and not the bad. He saw the positive and expanded on that! Most people seek change and personal growth. But self-actualized people are fulfilled.

Maslow says this regarding self-actualization, "'It refers to the person's desire for self-fulfillment, namely, to the tendency for him to become actualized in what he is potentially. The specific form that these needs will take will, of course, vary greatly from person to person. In one individual, it may take the form of the desire to be an ideal mother. In another, it may be expressed athletically; and in still another, it may be expressed in painting pictures or inventions' (Maslow, 1943, p. 382–383)." Know that this journey is just that, a journey, more so than a state of being.

In 1970, Abraham Maslow estimated that only two percent of people reach self-actualization. Whether that number still stands, I don't know. Don't let this discourage you, though. You could be one of the few!

He perceived 18 people to be self-actualized and made a note of 15 characteristics of a self-actualized person. These characteristics are as follows:

1. They perceive reality efficiently and can tolerate uncertainty;
2. Accept themselves and others for what they are;
3. Spontaneous in thought and action;
4. Problem-centered (not self-centered);
5. Unusual sense of humor;
6. Able to look at life objectively;
7. Highly creative;
8. Resistant to enculturation, but not purposely unconventional;

9. Concerned for the welfare of humanity;
10. Capable of deep appreciation of basic life experience;
11. Establish deep satisfying interpersonal relationships with a few people;
12. Peak experiences;
13. Need for privacy;
14. Democratic attitudes;
15. Strong moral/ethical standards.

But some of you may be wondering how you can get there if you lack those qualities but wish to become a self-actualized person. The following are behaviors that lead up to becoming a self-actualized person. They are as follows:

(a) Experiencing life like a child, with full absorption and concentration;

(b) Trying new things instead of sticking to safe paths;

(c) Listening to your own feelings in evaluating experiences instead of the voice of tradition, authority, or the majority;

(d) Avoiding pretense ('game playing') and being honest;

(e) Being prepared to be unpopular if your views do not coincide with those of the majority;

(f) Taking responsibility and working hard;

(g) Trying to identify your defenses and having the courage to give them up.

Knowing this, you can start to work on yourself and address areas in your life that may need some aid or improvement. Keep in mind that even Abraham Maslow knew that 'there are no perfect human beings.' It's important to remember this because no matter how hard we try, we are all human, and it's so important to try to do your best. Even though we try our best, there will be times in which we fall short, and that's okay.

Is Your Work and Home Environment Stimulating Creativity?

"You can't use up creativity. The more you use, the more you have." -Maya Angelou

You may not realize it, but light, color, sound, furnishings, and even more add to or take away from your creativity. You want to make sure that you are doing all you can to maximize your creativity and get all you can out of your environment. And if you can't afford to overhaul your space completely, that's fine. But perhaps, you can take these things I will teach you and start implementing them over time. By introducing these things to your work and home environment, you should see changes in your overall creativity, happiness, and health.

A scientific study proved that blue allows us to feel more comfortable and generates creativity more than red does. Which was shocking to me because I thought it would be the opposite. So, if you have an art room or a meeting space or an office perhaps, you should consider painting it blue, even if it's just an accent wall.

When you set your office up, your creativity is boosted if you face a room rather than face a wall. If you must face the wall, perhaps paint that wall blue and use artwork and natural elements to help spruce up the space and enhance creativity. Facing the space is a great way to feel comfortable, in control, and open to the room.

Put your walls to work. Make a chalk wall or a wall that can be used as a whiteboard. One weird thing that I learned is when your hands get creative, you get creative! Another significant aspect of having a chalkboard or a whiteboard on your walls is that it forces others to use it too! It's tempting and too hard not to! Therefore, you start to see multiple people collaborating on ideas, tasks, and projects.

Biophilic Design says that you should use lots of natural materials and abundant natural light. It also helps to incorporate plant products into your space. Especially flowers. Flowers make both men and women happy, and they smell fantastic too! That old saying, "take time to stop and smell the roses", is so true. It puts you in a great mood and grounds you in the present moment.

Add any sounds that might mimic those sounds that you hear in nature. For instance, birds chirping, water falling, rain or thunderstorms, etc. Ulrich in 1983, said that biophilic design helps to reduce stress and improve overall human health and happiness.

Nature has the same effect on your creativity and the creativity of others that it does on your overall health and happiness. Having plants in your workspace can boost creativity. If you are surrounded by nature, you will find yourself less stressed, and a less stressed mind is a more creative mind. As I type this, I listen to the birds chirping outside my window and admiring my pretty pink flowers.

Something that also helps is if you can get saccadic eye movement going. That helps strengthen both hemispheres of your brain, and it helps form new neural pathways between the two hemispheres. That gets your brain active and engages your whole brain, and will be a good lead into some creative ideas.

A bright room with lights like a classroom is not what you want for optimal creative thinking. A supermarket's lighting is often too much. The recommended amount for reading is too much, and so is your average office. For optimal creativity and spark in ideas you want an illumination of right around 150lx. That is dim. Perhaps the dimmer light makes you feel as if you are not being watched, and you feel more at ease to be vulnerable and be yourself.

Increased illumination also increases stress because, as individuals, we feel as if we are being watched. When people feel at ease, then their minds can be creative.

The sound/music optimal for creativity is what you would hear in your regular café on a busy day. Quiet is not the most optimal for creativity and ideas. I think this is like the fact of lighting. Too much quiet or too much lighting makes us feel like we are exposed. Feeling tense and stressed stifles creativity. We are most creative when comfortable.

Round tables are better for creativity and making participants feel as if their voice is valued and as if they are equal. It makes individuals feel as if there is a similar playing field. Whereas rectangular tables don't. They make one or more people feel as if they have all the power, and others feel uncomfortable, shy, or unsure if they should speak up and express their thoughts and ideas. That is something to think about when designing your office if you want to make people feel included.

Two things that help boost creativity are things that you can decorate your walls with. They are less focused artwork (pictures from farther away rather than zoomed in) and travel posters. Perhaps, it's actually "looking at the bigger picture" that gets our creative juices flowing. Travel posters or pictures are great because it makes us seem as if we are more worldly, experienced, and accomplished.

They release positive vibes and positive energy that allow ideas to flow. So, perhaps if you have a Paris poster laying around somewhere, you should get it up on your wall!

It's okay to take breaks from time to time to play or take a nap (yes, I said what I said.) Napping during the day gives your brain a break, and meanwhile, it is still working on solving all of your problems! Play is good too. A good reset for the body and mind. Sometimes, I believe play can help us develop solutions to our problems by relating the games we play to relationships, business, or other areas that might be causing us grief.

Another thing that I found interesting that helps boost your creativity is curved furniture. Curved furniture is more apt to get your creative juices flowing than furniture with straight lines! That makes me think about bunk beds made of Amish wood, my bedroom set, my recliner, and sitting in different chairs inside my house instead of the others. It makes sense when you think about it!

Critics & Their True Talents

"Unhappy people criticize. Happy people praise."
-Marisa Peer

When people criticize, it reflects what is going on inside them. They have something inside them that needs to be addressed and worked on.

For me to write this book and act as if you won't encounter critics, naysayers, and cynics, on your way to achieving your success and the highest version of yourself is a crock of crap. Odds are, unfortunately, you will. There will be people who try to steal your light because they have lost theirs. There will be people who will be downright mean to you, and you have never done anything to them.

I believe that they are jealous, like most of our mothers would say. They may not know that's what they are, but they see something in you that they want but don't have and can't figure out how to manifest. So, since they can't have it for themselves, they don't want you to have it either. But the good news is, (even though your light and kindness and happiness, etc., is invisible) they can only take it from you if you give it to them.

That is the tricky part. Holding on to your light when the dementors come to feast can be challenging. Just know that if they can take it from you, don't blame them. Things happen. But we always have the choice of how we will react. And I have found that this is easier said than done. Don't point fingers and say that they made you do anything. How you react is entirely up to you.

When you love yourself and believe that you are intelligent, kind, and have confidence in yourself, when these people come for you, it will be harder for them to get under your skin. When they send their attacks, they will bounce off, and you will realize that you don't have to accept their statements, actions nor let them in. It's a beautiful feeling.

You will begin to see that happy people won't try to steal your light. Instead, you will find that they are showering you with compliments every time you're around them, and they make you want to go out and take on the world! You want to be this person. People remember this person. This person always wins. Maya Angelou always said, "I've learned that people will forget what you said, people will forget what you did, but people will never forget how you made them feel." Let people remember you as the person who always came to them with good vibes, as the person that always lifted their spirits, and let someone else be remembered as the dementor!

We spend so much time in a negative space. We become caught up because someone said something rude to us or treated us unkindly. Don't get me wrong; I have been guilty of falling into this negative space myself, more than I care to admit. But negativity, anger, sadness, and the like only attracts more of the same.

Have you ever had a bad day that just seemed to get worse and worse? On the other hand, have you ever had a great day that just continues to get better and better, and you feel like you're on cloud nine? That's not a coincidence. That's the law of attraction. So, it's essential to be positive and take the high road. Don't let people steal your peace and your light. Don't let people make you act out of your character. Stay true to who you are and let your light stabilize you on solid ground.

You more than likely won't have this kind of stability overnight. You need to work on yourself. Praise yourself every day. Tell yourself you are enough. Tell yourself that you are beautiful, smart, generous, and kind. Tell yourself that you are lovable and that you love yourself. Be your own best friend. If you don't praise yourself, you may not receive the praise necessary to transform your life from someone else. So, do yourself a favor and shower yourself with compliments and positive affirmations daily!

Take the parts of yourself that you don't like and learn to accept them and love them! If you focus on your future and get excited about all the beautiful things to come, good things will come your way!

Don't ever change who you are for a partner or a job. It hurts your soul! The person who is meant for you will love you deeply and accept you for who you are. And until you find that person, DON'T COMPROMISE! NEVER PUT YOURSELF ON SALE. Wait for that person!

If your job wants you to compromise your integrity or morals, THAT IS NOT THE JOB FOR YOU. I once had a boss who asked me to lie to the venue's representative that we had recently used to make a minor issue that we had a MAJOR problem. I did not want to lie, and I am ashamed to admit that I did, so that I could keep my job. But it was then that I knew that getting a discount on the venue price for him was not worth the lie, and I also knew that the role I was in wasn't for me, and I would be leaving as soon as I could get something in place.

It's like that Little Big Town song, *Happy People*. Great song. If anyone from that band ever gets ahold of this book, I just want to say thank you for making fabulous music through the years. You have touched the lives of many, including mine. In the song, the lyrics say, "Happy people don't cheat. Happy people don't lie. They don't judge or hold a grudge, they don't criticize. Happy people don't hate. Happy people don't steal. 'Cause all the hurt sure ain't worth all the guilt they feel." I love this so much, and I can honestly say that if you are wondering about what happy people DON'T do this is a great song to reference.

Don't spend your energy trying to get over on someone or sabotage them or get revenge (I have a section about revenge in the book.) It's not worth it. Use your energy and mental capacity for only good and let karma or God or whatever you believe in handle the rest.

"Hurt people hurt people. Damaged people, damage people." -Marisa Peer

"Let it destroy you or let it motivate you." -Anna Egres

Before I started writing, I was living in the Nashville area and working for a company that had an office in this large office building. All the bathrooms on the floor were down the hall. There was a cleaning lady that I said, "Hi," almost every day and thanked her for keeping the building in tip-top shape.

One day I was in the ladies' room, and she told me that I had put on a lot of weight! When I said, "Excuse me?" She merely repeated herself over and over. The woman probably told me that I had packed on the pounds about five times! It was so rude of her. I didn't think I was fat at all. I was a size 6!

A similar situation occurred with a man in my apartment complex. His verbal attack was hurled at me while I was walking, trying to get some sun and some exercise. I thought both attacks were rude, uncompassionate, and uncalled for.

In the past, my weight has fluctuated quite a bit. For them to compare me to what I looked like three years ago was ridiculous and uncaring to me. I would like to take the time now to say that we are all beautiful and unique. We come in many shapes and sizes. What's important is for us to stay healthy and maintain a healthy lifestyle. The numbers on the scale and the size of your dress/shirt/pants, etc., don't matter. What matters is that you are healthy and happy.

In a perfect world, I would tell you that I was completely unaffected by the rude comments others have hurled at me my entire life, but that would be a lie. And until I get to the point where these comments don't hurt me anymore, and I can remain unchanged by the words, and actions of others, I've decided that I will use their negativity to fuel me. I will use their rude comments to motivate me and propel me to become a higher version of myself.

I made myself a goal (when the man in my apartment complex told me I wasn't in tip top shape, as if I didn't already know, I was not able to run like I used to.) I told myself I would train for two months then run a 10k. I found that just like how I don't practice my music if I don't have a target to aim at, I also don't train if I don't have a race.

Like I said, I would like for their comments to not affect me. But they did. They pissed me off. So, this summer when I am at the pool looking like the Italian version of J-Lo, they can eat their hearts out!

So, keep in mind that you can't always control what happens to you, but you can control how you react. I could (and I did for a couple hours. Being honest here.) choose to wallow in self-pity because someone called me fat. I could be completely unaffected by it and kill them with kind words. I could laugh and go about my day. But because I wasn't secure enough in myself at the moment, I used it as motivation and a kick in the pants to get me running and working out like I used to.

I think I mentioned earlier in the book that friends of my parents laughed in my face when I told them of my dream of being a singer, as a child. Well, whether you find me bootylicious or not, I can sing and can sing well. So, I guess the joke is on them and if they are ever in town, I will totally kick their butts in a karaoke competition!

One thing I learned is critics are only really good at one thing, BEING CRITICS. I don't know if they gave up on their dreams because someone discouraged them, but the dream killers are out there. They will try to rain on your parade and make you think that you can't be the Rockstar that you are. Don't let that stop you! Work hard, focus and never stop! You can be, do or have anything you want. I get that saying from Abraham Hicks! I have repeated it aloud and read it so many times that I think it's ingrained in my brain.

The sad part about it is the higher you rise; I feel like the more haters you get. Inside I think they are frustrated and can't figure out how it is that you are living your dream, speaking your truth, are happy and full of love and they are not. I think it's crazy when people try to ridicule people who are just trying to make the world a better place! Promise me today, that unless the criticism is constructive you will try to slow the spread of unknowingly hating and the discouragement of people, things and organizations that are just trying to accomplish improvement and betterment of our society and our world.

And remember above all else, that a critic's talent lies in critiquing. Don't listen to them. And if you can't not listen, then use their comments or actions to become the best you that you can be. And NEVER, EVER, EVER put your energy into revenge, especially, revenge that can physically harm another person or their property. Redirect that energy. Put that energy back into YOU so YOU can be all that YOU can be. Focus inward. Change you. Always be working on you. You are not in control of the other person.

Be Disciplined

"The key to your life is finding a vision that imposes discipline on you. In essence, vision is the source of discipline." -Dr. Myles Monroe

"Discipline is the root of leadership. It actually is the very nature that attracts people to you. A disciplined person naturally begins to attract people because people admire discipline in other people. That's why we go to see athletes perform. We really admire the discipline that they put themselves through." -Dr. Myles Munroe

"People trust a person that they perceive to be disciplined." -Dr. Myles Munroe

These are all great words given to us by the late and great Dr. Myles Munroe. I love how he links vision to discipline. I think the two are directly correlated because you can't have one without the other. People who lack vision, lack discipline and vice versa.

If you have a dream or goal (a vision) for your life you will be willing to sacrifice and put off pleasures for the sake of your dream. People who lead undisciplined lives don't have a clear and definite purpose or direction in which they are heading, so they can allow themselves to be undisciplined. You can't do that if you have a clear, definite purpose, a vision and dreams because if you don't discipline yourself you have to deal with the pain of not achieving your goals.

Dr. Myles mentioned that we admire discipline in other people. And when you take time to think about it, we really do. We go to see Beyoncé perform, knowing that as a child she didn't get to experience the same things other children were because she was practicing and competing in talent competitions like Star Search. He mentions athletes. I know, Michael Jordan had to meet his coach in the morning for early practice for practically a year before he made his high school basketball team. Now, most people wouldn't have put in the time or effort required. They wouldn't wake up early to go to practice when they aren't even on the team. That takes discipline. I've heard of some Olympians training twice on Christmas day just because the competition isn't and that will give them a leg up.

It's not always easy to discipline yourself, especially when your peers are whispering in your ear and tempting you to do things that you told yourself that you weren't going to engage in if you want to accomplish your goals. I have been offered drugs many times, but I always turn them down now because they don't aid me in getting to where I want to go in life. They would hinder and disrupt the process if not take over. I turn down a lot of offers to hang out or go out drinking after work.

Spending hours at the bar when I could be practicing my vocal technique, writing a new song, writing pages in my book, going for a walk or run, or spending quality time with the people I truly love, seems like a waste of my time. Not to mention the time and money you waste by getting a DUI (yes, I am telling you from experience, not a good idea.) Also, you put people's lives at risk including your own.

Leading a life of discipline is not always as exciting as it sounds. It sounds much more appealing and looks more alluring to live in that party atmosphere with sins and pleasures. However, most successful people lead highly disciplined lives and only allow themselves to indulge seldomly and when they do even that has its limits.

Dr. Munroe said that when you buy items with famous athlete's names on them or items in which they sponsor, you are really buying their discipline. And that makes sense. A lot of people do not have that discipline for themselves and cannot control themselves enough to ever have it so they try to purchase it from highly successful people that they aspire to be like.

"Vision simplifies life." -Dr. Myles Munroe

He says your vision will make your life become narrow and it won't be cluttered or filled with things. You will shake off or shed all those things that will not help you to get where you are going.

Your life will be simple and plain. But that isn't a bad thing.

"Once you know where you are going you also automatically know what roads won't take you there." -Dr. Myles Munroe

This is vital! That's what people are referring to when they say not all distractions are bad. Just because something is a good opportunity doesn't mean it's a good opportunity for you. Is it helping you get closer to your goal? Is it aiding you in your endeavors or is it wasting your time? A lot of us get stuck on the hamster wheel and we think we are really making progress when in reality, we are just running in circles going nowhere. Know what roads bring you closer to your goal and which roads don't.

"Your destiny dictates your decisions." -Dr. Myles Munroe

People who have vision and purpose live longer and lead healthier lives. If you know what's for you, you know what's not for you. And that just doesn't apply to opportunities and objects but that goes for people too. It's okay to lead a life that is simple and focused and not scandalous like reality shows. Focus on your goals. Focus on the one thing that sets your soul on fire. And stop getting distracted by all the temptations that are trying to delay or prevent progress towards your goals.

What are the necessary actions you need to take to bring you closer to accomplishing your dreams and goals? Not everything that is necessary for you to do will be fun. A lot of times delayed gratification needs to be implemented.

Not every book and seminar, book, webinar, networking event is for you. It's great that you may be attending these things, showing up and putting in the work. But not everything is for you. Find out what is for you and engage in that.

"You become a leader when you find the thing you are supposed to master. Everything that you do is supposed to be motivated by your vision." -Dr. Myles Munroe

"Vision helps you identify yourself." -Dr. Myles Munroe

Make yourself valuable in a certain area, Munroe says, so when people think about that they associate it with you. For instance, he gives the example, when you think of Barbra Streisand you think of her amazing singing voice and you think of her films and brilliant acting. It's important that you discipline yourself so you can excel and master a certain area. When people think of you, what do they think?

I really don't know how anyone can know true happiness (which I will touch on in the next section) without self-discipline. Without self-discipline you give in to the vices of life and you become average. If you are okay with average that's fine but I believe you were born to be extraordinary and change the lives of many.

There are many distractions that life throws at us to keep us from reaching our goals such as: over usage of social media, toxic relationships, unsafe sex (whether that is mentally, physically or emotionally), overindulgence when it comes to food, alcohol, taking drugs or things of the like.

Some may call me a prude or boring or no fun for all the things I won't allow myself to engage in or for some of the things I do. I honestly can tell you that there is no way in hell that I could live the life I am living today if I behaved in the manner that I used to.

When you practice self-discipline, it instills within you, a sense of pride, confidence and accomplishment. And if you can get yourself addicted to this feeling, that comes as a result of self-discipline, it would be extremely beneficial for you and your life and your probability of success.

The world will always be tempting us with temporary thrills and pleasures that seem irresistible but in the long term create pain, heartbreak, and lead to financial ruin. Don't give in to this. Decide how you are going to live your life. And if you decide to give in to appropriate vices. Do so in moderation. It's okay for you to have a glass of wine or two if you aren't driving but I would not recommend getting drunk every day of the week. That is not the path to wealth, abundance, or the highest version of yourself.

You must be strong willed enough to not give in to peer pressure and not do things just because everybody else is doing it. You must not say yes, every time someone offers you, or offers you to engage in behavior that you know is not good for you. And I know I sound like most moms in America right now, but seriously. Have some backbone and stop worrying about being cool or being liked. If the people who are asking you to engage in something in which you rather not either they aren't your friends or you haven't told them your boundaries so they can respect them.

Stand up for yourself. It's okay to be different. Tony Robbins always says that if you want to create lasting change or do/manifest something different in your life you must "raise your standard." If you make your new standard, I don't drink alcohol just think of all the things you can get accomplished when you aren't hungover. And I'm not saying, you must give up alcohol. Simply enjoy life by engaging in things within moderation and do what works for you.

Every day you are not going to FEEL like doing what's necessary for you to reach your goals. You are not going to FEEL like working out. You are not going to FEEL like making that extra sales call. Well, I got to tell you something, you are going to have to do it anyway. Stop making excuses for why you shouldn't do things that are going to better your life! Consistency will beat talent. One fault of mine is I don't practice music as much as I should. When I was growing up I practiced all the time. When I was in college, I practiced like crazy. But adulthood was different. When you are bombarded by all these things you need to do to be *responsible* and pay the *bills, sometimes* you get lost and things that truly matter to you get put on the backburner. So, I found out that I practice when I have a deadline and will excuse myself from practice when I don't. One great trick that I made up for me, so I can become more disciplined when it comes to practicing my music is giving myself deadlines. Whether the deadline is real or fake I psych myself into believing it, so I will put in the practice hours.

  Mel Robbins has a great solution to procrastination, her *5 Second Rule*. And if you are someone who has never seen her Ted Talks or read her book, I highly suggest you do. She says in the morning when your alarm clock goes off and you don't want to get up, count backwards from five, just like they do when a rocket goes off and your "blastoff" will be you getting yourself out of bed. She claims if you count backwards from five it will work every time and she has it backed by science. I will also tell you that it works every time because I do it too. I am a pretty motivated person but there are days when doing what I need to do is hard for me too.

Dwayne "The Rock" Johnson has an extremely disciplined workout/early morning routine. It's hard to believe that it doesn't contribute to his success as a pro-wrestler and actor. You can tell by looking at him that he just doesn't work out when he *feels* like it. To him it's a way of life.

He gets up every day at 4:00am and is doing a cardio workout by 4:30/4:45. When he wakes up it is still dark outside and then he will go and do strength training at a gym for about an hour and then he will start his work day, whether that be on the set of a movie or what have you. He says, "If you do anything, you never want to do anything half assed, especially when it comes to your training, get in, be intense, execute on it and get out." I really like his extreme discipline and the fact that he is one of those athletes that took their success as an athlete and made it a lifelong career. I really admire him for that. And just know that you don't have to be Dwayne to do this. You can implement changes in your life and have a morning routine, too. If you do, I promise you it won't be long before you start seeing results.

Happiness

"Where fear is, happiness is not."
-Lucius Annaeus Seneca

Happiness is a big deal when it comes to success. Happy people are magnetic. People want to be around them. And when you are magnetic you start to attract people in which you can start to form and build relationships with; business, personal, romantic, charitable, etc. So it's in your best interest to get happy if you are not happy. Maybe you need to work on putting a plan in place so you can slowly work towards getting out of that job that you hate. Maybe you need a little more sunshine. Maybe it means getting more exercise, a 20-minute walk on your lunch break. Or maybe it means learning to care a little less about what everyone else thinks. Maybe it means getting up earlier or scheduling some more "me time" into your weekly plans. Perhaps, it means getting a new hobby or picking up an old one that you think isn't "practical" for you to do anymore.

The weirdest thing that you will probably read in this entire book is the following, you know the whole *fake it 'til you make it* saying? Well, turns out it's true. One thing you could do to improve your overall happiness or get yourself to be happy is to trick your brain! Look in the mirror and say to yourself, "I'm so happy! I'm so happy! I am so happy! Thank you for this day! Thank you! Thank you! Thank you!" Or something very similar. Do this every day and do these multiple times a day. The repetition will help trick your brain into believing that you really are happy. Then one day you will wake up and you simply won't be faking it anymore.

Stop blaming others or events for why you are not happy. Every day we are given is a precious gift and what we decide to do with it is our ultimate 'Thank you' for getting the privilege to be here on this wonderful earth for another day. I had a vocal coach of mine who posted this quote on Facebook and I absolutely fell in love with it because it is so true. "If you could kick the person in the pants responsible for most of your trouble, you wouldn't sit for a month." -Theodore Roosevelt. THIS IS SO TRUE. Stop letting other people run your life. Stop focusing so much on what other people are doing and how they are behaving. Ask yourself what you are doing. Ask yourself what talents of yours, are you wasting? How could you put these talents to use to better serve yourself and others? "The secret to living is giving." -Tony Robbins

Perhaps, you are unhappy because you aren't giving enough. It's amazing what some time volunteering can do. Go to your local rescue mission and donate your time! Go feed a family who can't afford it. Go and donate your clothes that you don't wear anymore! Go and help out at your local animal shelter! Animals need lovin' too! Find something you can do to contribute. If you just change one life, it was all worth it! Help an elderly woman cross the street. Open the door for people and smile and gesture for them to go ahead of you. I'm telling you; a little kindness goes a long way and whatever you give, you get back in tenfold. I promise.

However, if you think you are depressed in the sense that you need to see a mental health professional. Please, seek professional help. I see that bumper sticker on the back of cars all the time, "It's okay to not be okay." It's okay to not be shitting sunshine and rainbows out your ass every single day. Also, if you are having suicidal thoughts PLEASE TELL SOMEONE. YOU ARE NOT ALONE! If you need to call the National Suicide Prevention Lifeline. It is 1-800-273-8255. All your loved ones want you here and alive and healthy and living your best life. So, please do not be afraid to tell someone you are struggling.

I really hope that some of these tricks I have brought to light (many of them you have probably heard of before) help you and change the trajectory of your entire life. If I make an impact on you after reading this, please reach out and let me know. That is what I am doing this for. To encourage you and inspire you. And let you know that we create our reality. And that people are mostly good. There's a quote by Abraham Hicks that I have on the bottom of my email that I believe in with every fiber of my being, it goes like this, ""Welcome to Planet Earth. There is nothing that you cannot be, or do, or have. You are a magnificent creator." That just inspires me to go after my goals and dreams with a force that has never been seen before! And although sometimes I fall short (let's admit it, we're all human) I know deep down in my soul that I will get where I am going! You can too. Be happy. Be thankful! Be present!

Have Clear Set Boundaries

"Lack of boundaries invites lack of respect."
~ Anonymous.

Having no boundaries is a recipe for disaster. You are setting yourself up to fail. Without clear and concise boundaries, people will walk all over you, take you for granted, and mistake your kindness for weakness. It's important not to let people do this to you.

I have seen this in my own life and the lives of my friends when it comes to romantic relationships, business affairs, kids, and so on. If you don't have clear set boundaries, you feel like a doormat, used and underappreciated. Lovers will come and go as they please and only come around and stay when beneficial to them. When it's not, they leave you in tears and wondering what you did and why you aren't good enough to please and keep them.

Well, you are good enough. But you haven't laid out what's acceptable and unacceptable. If you have a business and are available 24 hours a day, that's great, and all, but your customers are taking advantage of you. Do you need to develop business hours and hours where you wish not to be contacted? Maybe you need quality time with your family to be undisturbed by customers. Don't let anyone violate that. You have a right to do what's best for you.

It is not rude or mean to have boundaries. You need to be able to stick to them! Don't ever fall prey to peer pressure if someone is pressuring you to make an exception and let you or them break your boundaries. Don't do it. They are there to protect your mental, physical, and emotional health.

Think about a castle with a mote and a stone wall around it. The people who reside within the castle have the mote with the alligators or piranhas to safeguard the castle. And that's what your clear set boundaries are there for to guard you and your wellbeing.

If someone wants to be in your life, such as a romantic partner or prospective client, they will respect your boundaries if you communicate with them clearly. If someone disrespects you or your limits, you may have to consider that you may be better off without them.

"When we fail to set boundaries and hold people accountable, we feel used and mistreated." ~ Brené Brown.

Often, if you feel this way, you need to look at yourself and not at the other person. People treat you how you teach them to treat you (a saying that I remember Dr. Wayne Dyer would use.) Maybe that person you're dealing with isn't intentionally treating you in such a way that results in you feeling abused and mistreated. Perhaps, if you started setting boundaries with that person, they would respect them, and you wouldn't feel that way any longer. Just know that the problem isn't always the other person, and you don't have to cut people out of your life at first. First, start by implementing what your limits are and then see what they do after. Their behavior following the creation of your boundaries and you sticking to them (cause trust me, people will test them to make sure you are going to stick to them) is when you will see if they are meant to or not meant to be in your life.

One thing to be careful of is making sure your boundaries only include you and not the other person. You do not want to control or manipulate another person. The only person that you can change is yourself. So, make sure your boundaries are just for you and go about expressing them to others in a manner that is not aggressive but instead is kind, firm, and polite.

There is an excellent book on boundaries that if you haven't read and are having trouble in that department, I recommend you check it out. It is called, *Boundaries, When to Say Yes, How to Say No to Take Control of Your Life* by Dr. John Townsend & Dr. Henry Cloud.

The book mentions something that a lot of us encounter one time or another in our professional lives, being overwhelmed at work because not only are you doing your job, but you are also doing your co-workers. A story talks of an administrative assistant who works on travel arrangements and those kinds of details for guest speakers and her co-worker who is supposed to set up the food and physical items for the event. The admin is feeling overwhelmed because she keeps taking on her co-workers' responsibility. He keeps asking her if she doesn't mind, so she does it.

Someone approaches her, and she talks to them about what's been bothering her at work, and they tell her not to save him and do his work for him next time he comes to her with a request to do his job for him. So, she listens and goes along with the advice. She declines his requests to take on the extra work, and when the event isn't set up how it needs to be, the boss blames her co-worker and not her, and the administrative assistant no longer feels overwhelmed and stressed.

Boundaries are helpful in many areas of our lives. And if you are a people pleaser like me, they can be hard to learn. I am still working on it. But I am getting better. For those out there who struggle with this, I will say this, setting boundaries is not being mean. I repeat, SETTING BOUNDARIES IS NOT BEING MEAN!

The Power of "I Am"

"Whatever follows the "I am" will eventually find you." - Joel Osteen, The Power of I Am: Two Words That Will Change Your Life Today

I love this quote above by Joel. He truly realizes the power in those two short words. Whatever follows those two short words is what you will likely become, so be careful about what follows. You want to only speak about things that you want to manifest. Perhaps, you have been saying things that have gotten you into the situation you are in now. And if you don't like the situation that you are in now, let me tell you, it all starts with our thoughts and our words, and our words then become actions and our actions become habits and soon all that forms into beliefs. Our beliefs seem to be what is at the core of who we are. So, be careful what you say following "I am" it will bring about something you will thank or kick yourself for!

In the Old Testament of the bible, Moses asks God what he shall call Him, and God replies, "I am that I am." I learned a lot about the power of 'I am' from the late and great Dr. Wayne Dyer. I have done his "I am" meditations plenty of times and listened to him talk about the power of what you put behind those two words. It's incredible the power that they have. Most people don't even realize it, and they say the most self-deprecating thing, and then wonder why things aren't going as well as they had hoped! LISTEN TO HOW YOU ARE TALKING TO YOURSELF. Whatever name you have for the divine, you are a divinely created being, and living here in this fabulous time/space reality. Do you think that any creator of yours wants to hear you talk about yourself like, "I'm fat." Or "I'm stupid." Or "I'm a drunk, and I'll always be drunk because my daddy was that way."

    Oh, my land! No wonder things aren't going according to plan! Would you talk to your best friend that way? Probably not. If you did, you wouldn't be a very good friend! So, tell me, why are you talking to yourself that way?

    "When negative thoughts come, the key is to never verbalize them." -Joel Osteen, The Power of I Am: Two Words That Will Change Your Life Today

    Take and defeat those negative thoughts by not breathing life into them. When you speak things, you don't wish to come to pass, you give them life to grow. But the same is true of the opposite! And guess what? It takes the same amount of work! So, tell me, why not set yourself up for success by only talking positive and good things into existence? I think you will find yourself happier, healthier, and more successful if you do.

I swear, I almost 'get high' from repeating over and over my positive "I am" affirmations. I can feel the energy in my body change. I can feel myself smiling from my eyes. I can't help it! Keep in mind that we are all energy and everything you believe to know is energy! It's essential to raise your level of vibration because then you will begin to attract more things that are vibrating at that same level!

You need to praise yourself! Say things like, "I am patient. I am kind. I am a spark of the divine. I am a student of the world. I am peace. I am light. I am empathetic. I am a giver." Doesn't that just sound better! Speak those words until they become true and stop it with the negative self-talk. Your creator would not appreciate the way you talk about yourself! Plus, it doesn't do any good. Do you think you will stop being drunk if you define yourself as a drunk and declare that you'll always be that way because your daddy was that way? Oh, my land! What a recipe for failure! Don't do that! Talk yourself up! Praise yourself! You can be so much more than what you are now! Believe in yourself! And be careful what you put after I am!

Your definition of yourself is what you will fulfill. So, be extra careful when defining yourself. You will either rise to the occasion or shrink to fit the smaller version you have cast yourself as.

"Words have a biochemical effect on the body. If you want to change your life, if you want to shape your decisions and your actions, shifting your emotional patterns are the key. One fundamental tool that can change it faster than anything else is consciously selecting the words you use to describe how you feel. That is how you create a level of choice instead of a habitual reaction. Simply by changing your habitual vocabulary (the words you consistently use to describe emotions), you can instantaneously change how you think, how you feel, and how you live." —Tony Robbins

Tony is right! Your words have the power to change your life radically. Maybe our parents were right when they told us to *watch our mouths!* Like I've said before in this book, one of the most incredible things about a lot of the material I cover in this book is it's free! Changing the way you speak to yourself and about yourself is free! Not letting negative thoughts escape from your bodily prison will be tough, at first but, that is free, too! And it can change your life! If you aren't doing this, why aren't you?

Having lousy language when it comes to how you speak to or about yourself negatively affects your overall health, something that you should consider.

Paula Owens, a holistic nutritionist, has an "I AM A-Z Exercise." This exercise consists of going through the alphabet and following "I am" with empowering words such as "amazing," "energized," "radiant," etc. Replace your negative descriptions with a positive. If you don't think you can eliminate your negative self-talk or how you have been defining yourself, I dare you to challenge yourself with this exercise. It will feel weird and foreign to say all these kind things about yourself if you aren't used to it. All I have to say is, get used to it! Do it over and over until you start to believe what you are saying to be true!

Be More in Love with Your Future Than Your Past

"Nothing we do can change the past, but everything we do changes the future." - Ashleigh Brilliant

People live a good chunk of their lives in their past and if you live in your past, more than likely, you will be stuck on a hamster wheel and will continue to recreate your past. You need to be so in love with your future that your history takes a backseat.

Dr. Joe Dispenza talks about this a great deal, and he says that there is evidence that your memories will begin to support the story you tell. So, they aren't as factual as you believe them to be, and you need to release their intense power over you. You must focus on who you want to be, not on who you were.

Often, living in our past leaves us broken down with bad memories and negative self-beliefs that we THINK we can't shake. Living in your future gives you hope and excitement for the possibilities of the life you can create and what awaits you ahead. At times, just the opposite happens. Some people are so in love with their past that they look at old photographs often and seem to be romancing their past. These people are escaping what lies ahead of them, as well.

People are often more than willing to tell you all about their past. Dr. Joe Dispenza points out that often when they tell you about their past, what they are saying is this event happened to me, and I haven't changed much, if at all since. So, we see stagnancy with people who live in the past. He also tells us that as time passes, we lose parts of our memories, and after some time 50% of the stories we are telling others about what happened isn't even the truth. They use this, most times, as an excuse for why they are not becoming what they set out to be.

We must teach people to be defined by a vision of the future, says Dispenza. We must start thinking differently than what we previously had and making different decisions. New ways of thinking, new experiences, new emotional states, and new actions can seem uncomfortable, unfamiliar, and uncertain. When you do this, life becomes somewhat unpredictable. Your body tries to influence your mind and take you back to your comfort and safe zone by discouraging these new actions, thoughts, and feelings. He says that people can change their gene expression within four days if they go at this with full force. A resistance to the old and a complete intoxication with the future that lies ahead of you that you have consciously decided to create.

95% of who you are at the age of 35 is a set of behaviors operated by your subconscious. To change, you need to overwrite that program.

The benefits of meditation have been experienced by many. If you haven't tried it, I suggest you give it a go.

Be Authentic – Be You

"Today you are You, that is truer than true. There is no one alive who is Youer than You." — Dr. Seuss, Happy Birthday to You!

Do not sacrifice who you are for anything. People can tell when you are not authentic. Your authenticity opens the flood gates to abundance and all the more incredible things in life. Why would you want to be anyone else? The mere chance of you being here is slim. It's truly a miracle.

I love Evan Carmichael on YouTube and when doing research for this book, I came across a video he had put together on being authentic. I think he is a perfect example of just that. His videos are viewed by thousands. He took something some people were already doing and made it entirely his own. He studies the masters in all areas of life, and now his channel has a net worth of over $619,000. All because he decided to follow his dream, go out on a limb, and do what makes him happy. You can tell how much he loves it. Thank you, Evan, for inspiring us every day! Your work is being noticed all around the globe!

Lady Gaga and her mother Cynthia, in 2012, founded the Born This Way Foundation or the (BTWF). Their goal is to create "a kinder and braver world." Its mission is as follows:

"*Born This Way* looks forward toward a future that supports the wellness of young people through an evidence-based approach that is fiercely kind, compassionate, accepting, and inclusive. We celebrate the individuality of those we serve, and we revere the bravery it takes to reach out and start the conversation. Together, we're building a community that provides approachable resources, fosters genuine connection, and drives action."

Lady Gaga had been bullied in school and growing up and I would imagine as a pop star, too. She knows what it is like to fiercely need to be you and the success that comes when you let go and decide to be yourself. You mustn't live in hiding or fear. There is always someone to talk to if this is how you are feeling. When you are not yourself, others take notice. When you are living in authenticity, people notice that, too. Which would you rather notice?

If you are interested in donating or getting involved with the Born This Way Foundation, please visit their website https://bornthisway.foundation/ and see what you can do to create a kinder and braver world. As always, I'd like to thank Lady Gaga and her mother, Cynthia, and all those who work at and donate to the foundation for all that they do. It's incredible what people can do!

Bob Proctor started after taking advice from his friend and mentor and drastically changed his income in one year. It took him nine years to describe what he did fully, and he wanted to share what he had learned with other people, but he was shy, he said. Bob Proctor, at the time, would get nervous just talking in front of 4 to 5 people. He had to learn to embrace who he was and his great news to have the courage to break through and share what he had learned with the world. He had to embrace his authenticity.

One day he was standing in the back of the O'Hare Hyatt Hotel ballroom watching Bill Gove speak, and he said something that changed Bob's life dramatically. Bill said, "If I wanna be free, I've gotta be me, not the me I think you think I should be, not the me I think my wife thinks I should be, not the me I think my kids think I should be. If I wanna be free, I've gotta be me." Then he said, "I better know who 'me' is."

Standing at the back of the ballroom, Bob found himself wanting more than ever to know who he was. He wanted to share what he had learned with the world so badly, but he was shy. Bob had listened to Earl Nightingale's recordings so many times. He knew that he had talent, and certain things were not only meant to be accomplished by the few but by whoever set their minds to it, focused on it, and worked towards it. Yet, he still had this block, it seemed, and was holding himself back from sharing what he had learned.

Bob Proctor made up his mind, then and there, that not only was he going to learn and master what Bill Gove was talking about that very day, but he was going to have him teach him, and he did. The two men became great friends! Gove taught Proctor to be comfortable in front of a camera and speaking in front of people whether the crowd was 50 people or a crowd of 20,000.

Gove said to him, "Bob, if you want to be effective, just think of the people you are talking to. Just fall in love with the idea of helping them." And then he said, "You can help them because you got valuable information." Those words were spoken to him 51 years ago at the time of this writing.

Bob didn't shake loose of his shyness right away. But over time, with some coaching, it left him. And if you can relate to this story because you consider yourself to be shy, too, it can leave you, as well. All you have to do is work on it. Proctor can now express himself freely, he says, and he isn't burdened with self-doubt.

Iyanla Vanzant talks about being authentic. She says you must become clear about who you are, about your purpose in this life, about what you're up to, and you speak the truth of that every day. When you are not authentic, you are living life at only a fraction of what you could be. Vanzant says that what you think, say, and do all have to align to live an authentic life. That is so true. When you take time to think about people whose thoughts, words, and actions don't align, we often are suspicious of them or don't consider them trustworthy. Most of the time, we never feel entirely comfortable around these people. There is always something about them that we can't quite put our finger on.

Vanzant says that as she travels all over, she witnesses people every day who are "suffering in silence", simply meaning that people suffer greatly when they don't allow themselves to be all they are. I know this feeling all too well. While living in Michigan with my parents while in high school and after college, before I moved to Nashville, I often felt frustrated and like I couldn't spread my wings. Don't get me wrong, I love my parents, and I would do anything for them as I'm sure they would do the same for me. But I was smothering part of my soul, my personality, and it wanted to come up for air. I don't know if it was the social part of me that I wasn't able to engage in full or the fact that my artistic soul just longed to be free. I was often easily agitated, and I think it was mostly because I wasn't living in the totality of who I was. Now, I don't experience that frustration or feel like I'm smothering parts of my personality.

Be true to who you are. Don't let others talk you into doing, thinking, or saying things that you don't believe. It's not good for your soul. I know you are thinking, *Anna, how will I know when I'm doing, saying, and acting in ways I don't believe?* All I can tell you is; you will know. Deep down inside you, you will know that whatever you are doing does not align with the core of who you are. And you will witness issues being birthed as a result of not being who you are, however big or small they may be.

Along with being authentic, we must also take into consideration the Law of Attraction. When we align with our higher selves and live and walk in our truth, we will attract like people. We will attract people that are honest and live with integrity and good morals. When you are not living your truth, you will attract people of the like, as well. Those people may want to deceive you, have ulterior motives, or have a hidden agenda.

That authentic spiel doesn't just go hand in hand with the individual, but it goes along with groups, organizations, and businesses. Many times, you will find a company that has a strong why. With a vital mission that it builds its business around, this business will usually have loyal customers. Companies that try to get on by following market trends and riding the wave of popular culture usually don't do as hot. Organizations such as non-profits do better when people are attracted to them because they like what they are doing and why they are doing it.

So, what you are seeing is a pattern. If you feel a little lost in life, I think you must be true to yourself first, live your authentic life, and then let the people who want to be in your life, be in your life. The people and things that are meant for you will embrace and accept the core of who you are, let the others fall to the side.

If you are struggling, another incredible thing you can do to live a more authentic life is to journal and look back at the last day, week, month, or year. See what you did that you were proud of and where were the areas in which you let yourself down. In what areas did you feel as if you weren't authentic? Don't get me wrong, I am usually the first person to say don't look to the past, focus on your future. But in this situation, I think that a little reflection can do us good. It kind of ties into the section of this book where I talk about comparing yourself to who you were yesterday. An authentic person will be, more than likely, focusing inward and trying to improve daily.

If you are having a hard time becoming courageous enough to live in the truth of who you are, ask yourself what your purpose is here. Once you figure that out, write it down somewhere where you can see and read it clearly. Remind yourself every day what mission the divine put at your feet to accomplish. Let that fuel you and motivate you and your actions. Operate with your purpose clearly defined in your heart and mind.

I know Oprah, when she first started as a reporter, was constantly trying to be like Barbara Walters, from stories she's told and speeches she's given. She said that she was on the air and reading the teleprompter one day, and she mispronounced Canada because she was trying to talk like Barbara. Oprah said she started laughing because it was so silly. Around this time, she realized she had to stop trying to be Ms. Walters and start being herself. Oprah is the prime example that being yourself is the ticket to success for yourself. I'm sure her success didn't come immediately after she stopped trying to be like Barbara, but it didn't come when she was.

My Barbara is Kim Kardashian. I think she is beautiful, kind, intelligent, and savvy. In my senior year of college, I always compared the guy I was with and I to Kim and Kanye. I wanted to be her. I wanted to live in her fancy house. And have a family like hers. I wanted her kids, vacations, and businesses.And some of you may roll your eyes because you may not like her, and that's fine, but I do, and I spent so much time and energy trying to be like her.

I don't anymore. I realized that I'm Anna Egres. I'm a spark of the divine. I'm an Italian/Croatian mixed European mut that looks more like her mother than her father (minus the fact that I didn't get her amazingly gorgeous olive skin). I sing and write songs and am a total nerd (you can usually find me reading or writing). And I'm not Kim. There's only one Kim Kardashian West, and there's only one Anna Egres. God wants me to be Anna Egres. The one he created me to be. God/The Universe doesn't want me to be Kim or Kim to be me. I will come into more great things in my life by simply being who I uniquely am. It is so important just to be who you are.

    Leo Gura will be the first to tell you that you are absolutely magnetic when you are in alignment and living in your truth. People will be more attracted to you and want to be around you. When I think of someone that fully embraces their authentic self, I think of Lizzo. I love her personality. When she walks into a room, it's all eyes on her. And when she performs it is so thrilling to watch her play her flute and incorporate in pop music something that was such a big part of her past.

    When you permit yourself to be your true self, you start to lead a life filled with happiness instead of full of anger, resentment, depression, frustration, or lies. You begin to worry less about what it may "cost" you to live the life you truly desire and more about the benefits that are associated with no longer "suffering in silence."

    If you are in a situation where you are not living an authentic life, picture yourself slowly changing your life and starting to live with your thoughts, words, and actions all aligning with your truth. Think of yourself shedding the old you like a snake sheds its skin and emerges anew, leaving the old skin behind and journeying onward.

Listen to the voice inside you, and don't let the fear of what others will say or do dictate how you live your life. You'll gain confidence when you say no to fear and when you dare to live in your truth no matter what it is that you find yourself doing or where you are at. You are special! You are unique! Your voices, talents and opinions deserve to be heard and seen! Don't let anyone ever try to take that away from you!

David Allen, the founder of the David Allen Company, says it takes people time for people to develop their signature. It takes time to establish what that is. I agree with him here wholeheartedly. I have many people that I aspire to be like, people who are older and wiser than myself.

I also saw this with the late and great Amy Winehouse. Many people know her for *Back to Black* and *Rehab*, her thick cat-winged eyeliner, and her black beehive. But a lot of pop music fans don't know about her debut album, *Frank*. Many people don't know that she didn't have the beehive and all the tattoos when she first started. She wasn't always as thin as she was during the height of her career, and that sound evolved out of her previous exposure to the jazz greats like Sarah Vaughn, Tony Bennet, Frank Sinatra, and Dinah Washington. Many people don't know that she loved girl groups from the 60s and wanted to make a record like that.

What Amy Winehouse is best known for took time. Her voice was always there, but the style and the fashion and the sound changed and evolved. It took her years to find her signature, as it may with you. Amy was a true original, and there will never be anyone on this earth that will ever be quite like her! I never met her, but I miss her dearly.

To be who you are, you must learn to love and accept yourself, flaws and all. Things will become easier, and you won't have to worry about the pressure of behaving a certain way. People will ask you how you did it! Be authentic! Be who you are! Live in your truth!

Get a Mentor/Coach

"A mentor is someone who allows you to see the hope inside yourself." -Oprah Winfrey

In 2019, I sought out a life coach named Becky Buckman, and she works in the Nashville area. I had never been to a life coach before but thought it was time because I needed to make some radical changes to my life. I was at a point where I was questioning how I was contributing to the world and why I wasn't earning more money. In our phone call before our meeting, I told Becky, "I am too talented not to be earning more money." To some of you, I may come across as self-absorbed. But I am not ashamed of that statement. I love myself, and am incredibly talented, and I deserve to be making more money using my talents.

I had gone to see Becky with the hope of breaking through my limiting beliefs surrounding money. Instead, I had a shocking revelation. When I was in the session, she asked me a series of questions/statements to find out more about me and where I was at. She said to me, "Men are…" and told me I had to answer with one word, and that word had to be the first word that popped into my head. I squinted my eyes, scrunched up my nose, and shook my head. I said to her, "Do I have to say the *first* word?" And she told me, yes, and the word fell out of my mouth with disappointment in myself, "Unavailable", I muttered.

    During our session, that day, I learned a lot more about myself, and I learned ways to work on changing my limiting beliefs and maintaining my peace in situations. I will admit that I did not do all of the homework that Becky gave. However, Becky and I have communicated since our session, and I thanked her for the beautiful breakthrough that I had that day thanks to her.

    I was having troubles in my dating life for quite some time, but I thought since it was so easy for me to get dates, it wasn't an issue, and sooner or later, I'd find my prince charming. I had no IDEA that I had this negative belief that men were UNAVAILABLE. Perhaps, that is why the men I dated would ghost me, leave me for other women, come in and out of my life, lie to me, and never treat me like I knew I deserved. When I realized this, I knew I had to find a mate differently and knew that I had to avoid those infamous pitfalls that I always found myself in. I started to change my behavior. Once I knew better, I had to do better.

    I had a professor in college that I still talk to regularly. I call him Doc. He has had a significant impact on my life as a professor, mentor, and friend. He is someone that I can look up to and try to model my life after. He is a great person and has taught me wonders not only about jazz and music in general but about life and the right way to treat people and overcome obstacles, as well. He is well-read and well-spoken. Doc tells me of books and articles I should read and videos and documentaries I should watch. He will tell me stories from his own personal experience that relate directly to what I am going through or trying to learn. He has a great way of teaching you but letting you do a significant amount of the learning on your own. He is more like a life guide in a sense. He means a great deal to me and will be the subject of my next book. He is like the uncle I always wanted but never had, and I am determined to tell the whole world about him and all the good he has done.

    Just know that even the masters have coaches and lean on them for advice. I know plenty of singers that are great at what they do. The average person would say that there is no reason for them to see a vocal coach, but they do, even if it is as little as once or twice a year. Many people don't know that the journey to mastery is a lifelong one, and you never actually get there. Dr. Paul Brewer, my former college professor, mentor, and friend I mentioned above, is a fantastic trombone player, to put it lightly, and a lifelong musician. He tells me that he is learning new things all the time, and when he was teaching at the college, he was constantly learning. He would even learn things from his students! And that's another great lesson to learn. Almost everyone you come into contact with can teach you something. But you must be open and able to accept the lesson which they provide.

Even all-star basketball players like Steph Curry have coaches. In an article by ESPN.com, *Inside the relationship that unleashed Steph Curry's greatness*, Steph Curry sends his praises to coach Bob McKillop and credits him with teaching him "everything" he knows. He gave him confidence, taught him the meaning of hard work, saw potential in him, and believed in him. He states, "He told me when I was a freshman that I had a license to shoot any shot I wanted, but I'd have to work for it. I'd have to put in the time and actually commit to learning on the job. Even when I failed early freshman year, he stayed in my ear because he saw my potential before I did."

Bob McKillop had a motto "Trust, Commitment, and Care." These are the kinds of values that he instills in his players. Steph took what he learned from McKillop and used it to propel him to great success. He taught him valuable morals and characteristics while encouraging him despite any failures of his or shortcomings. And this is what great mentors and coaches do. They see the best in you and try to extract it like gold from a mine. It is so crucial for you to have a great mentor/coach in your life.

Einstein, Tai Lopez revealed, had a mentor and would have lunch with him every Thursday growing up. Alexander, the Great, had Aristotle as a mentor. Bill Gates had Paul Allen as a mentor. Warren Buffet had Benjamin Graham.

Law of 33% - spend time with people that you are helping to mentor – they will make you feel good about yourself.

33% with people who are on your level - friends and peers.

The last 33% of your time is what people forget about – people who are 10-20 years ahead of you. "They will make you feel a little bit uncomfortable, but that's what you want, and remember you don't want to make the mistake most people make with mentors, finding somebody just a little bit better than them. You don't want to be the blind leading the blind. So, I call it the 10x rule; find somebody ten times further ahead than you. If you want to learn to grow a 1-million-dollar company, you have to find someone with a 10-million-dollar company. Don't be afraid to go to the top. In-person mentors are amazing. And you can get people like Warren Buffet, Bill Gates. You'd be surprised!"

"People remember their struggle, and they'll reach out and help you, too." – Tai Lopez

For Oprah Winfrey, her mentor was the late and great Maya Angelou. When Oprah told her that her Leadership Academy for girls in South Africa would be her greatest legacy, Maya corrected Oprah, "You have no idea what your legacy's gonna be," Oprah disagreed. Maya was in her kitchen, and Oprah said, "(Maya) put her dough down. She wipes her hands, and she points at me, and she says, 'I said you have no idea what your legacy will be because your legacy isn't one big thing. It may be the school or a part of it. It's not your name on a building or an African school. Your legacy is every life you touch."

That's just the thing. Most of the time, mentors are older and wiser than us and have experienced more life. They see things differently and can enlighten us and expand our way of thinking about ourselves, the world, and our possibilities. Oprah thought the school would be her most outstanding achievement, but Maya knew she was wrong. She was right when she said that *your legacy isn't one big thing*. The Oprah Show touched the lives of millions and helped raise generations of people. Oprah helped mold and instilled good moral values in people across the world, and that was just her getting started. She has so much more to accomplish and so much more she hopes to do. From the looks and sounds of it, she may be trying to start some more schools. Maya saw infinite possibilities and the potential for a far more incredible legacy than Oprah's vision, at that time, allowed her. I think now she understands exactly what it was that her friend, Maya, was getting at.

Mentors and coaches have a way of seeing us and what our future could be. Oprah has expressed how grateful she is for her time shared with Maya and how she misses her.

    If you don't have a mentor or coach in your life, please reach out to someone who specializes in your field who is where you would love to be. Or perhaps, look for people in your community (be careful of the limits you put on your community) that inspire and motivate you. Find someone who you admire who is well respected and who treats others with kindness and compassion. These people help shape us into who we are to become, and I don't know what we would do without them.

Find One Person Who Believes in You More Than You Believe in Yourself

"My father gave me the greatest gift anyone could give another person, he believed in me."
- Jim Valvano

One of my vocal teachers Margaret Rose believes in me sometimes even more than I believe in myself. She tells me what a fantastic voice I have and how I can do any genre and the only thing stopping me is my negative beliefs. She used to tell me when I would start going down the rabbit hole that my mental blocks were okay, and I could invite them in and sit with them and give them a chocolate bar. Ha-ha, and my blocks didn't have to be this huge thing. I could invite them in until they no longer came to visit me.

And what she did, the way she believed in me with such vigor and not a doubt in the world. That is one thing that I held onto when times got tough for me.

For Joel Osteen, it's his wife, Victoria. She encouraged him to Pastor Lakewood Church long before his father passed away, and he stepped up to the plate and took over. She thinks that he can do anything! She saw the potential in him before he even did!

It's so crucial for you to have someone like this in your life and keep them close to you! They will make your reach higher and achieve more. You will surprise yourself and accomplish what you've never even dreamed of simply because they were there by your side and they believed in you!

This one person may not be a family member, but for some of you, it may be someone as close to you as your mom. Remember to be careful who you share your dreams and goals with because not everyone will root for you.

But having someone who sees more than you see in yourself will constantly challenge you and keep you pushing onward when you experience tough times. They will challenge you to do things that you never thought yourself capable of, and they will do it lovingly.

You can usually differentiate these people from others because their energy will be different. When you are around them, you will feel elevated and like you are more than you currently are. They will make you feel unstoppable and like anything (with some hard work) is possible. These are the people that you want in your corner. You need to check in with this type of person when you find yourself experiencing self-doubt.

I believe that people are put in your life for a reason, season, or a lifetime. This person, who believes in you more than you believe in yourself, was put in your life by the divine to help catapult you to greatness. They are here to support and encourage you to become all you are and all you are meant to be.

Another thing you must remember is that YOU have the possibility of being this person to others. Don't count yourself out. If someone is doing this for you, know that you can return the favor by continuing the cycle of giving. Look for someone that you see massive potential in and a strong work ethic. Help encourage and support this person in their journey to accomplishing their hopes, goals, and dreams. Don't forget that you, too, can be a catapult for someone else, and they will forever be grateful to you.

You may not be believing in yourself because you are falling victim to comparison and doubting your capabilities. Just remember to only compare yourself to the person you were yesterday. Also, remember that you are a human capable of change and growth. Perhaps, you don't know everything you need to know or don't have all the skills you need to be successful in a particular area of your life. That's okay. You can learn and obtain these things. The person that believes in you more than you believe in yourself will see the ability you have to smash your goals and to seriously kick some butt, even though it may be difficult for you at this point. Keep in mind, that is why they are there.

Keep in mind that perception determines reality. What you perceive to be true about how others view you and your skills and knowledge and how you view your skills and knowledge can be changed. You don't have to think the way you always thought. Shift your thinking to positive and make sure you are not engaging in negative self-talk. Start having expectations of people receiving you more positively. Start expecting outcomes to play out in your favor. Tell yourself that people think highly of you and want what you have to offer.

No Time for Excuses

"If you really want to do something, you'll find a way. If you don't, you'll find an excuse." – Jim Rohn

Before he became wealthy, Jim Rohn had a reason for everything, so that he didn't look bad. Listening to his speeches over the years, I can almost repeat it word for word. But he said he blamed the government, taxes, prices being too high, the traffic, his car, the company he worked for, the training he received, the negative neighbors and relatives, the economy, the weather, and so on. I think this list is so funny because we all use these things as an excuse, and the thing is, none of that matters. His mentor told him there was a problem with his list of reasons; he wasn't on it. And it is kind of humorous when you think about it. But it's the truth! It's not what occurs in your life. It's how you react to those events. It is up to you. The difference between average and the people who achieve great things is how they respond to their life events. How they take the obstacles in their life, learn from them and use them to make them stronger.

Stop making excuses for why you can't accomplish your dreams and goals. Stop making excuses for why you aren't on a journey to becoming your highest self. The odds are you think that you are being and doing all you can, but you're not. Time to look at yourself in the mirror and see what areas of your life you can improve!

You may not know it, but many people thrive in a bad economy. And can you guess why? It's their mentality! They don't see it as a setback. They see it as a total advantage. It might be buying stocks at a low price or purchasing a home with a mortgage with an interest rate so low that they feel like they are stealing! People don't realize that your truth/reality is what you perceive it to be! Change your perception, and you can change not only your financial future but your destiny!

People often blame others for the shortcomings and failures in life, when in reality, you only have yourself to blame. I know that goes against the grain of my message of "be delusional", but you can own up to your shortcomings while being delusional at the same time.

Gary Vaynerchuk says many people's number one excuse is that they don't have any money. While that may be true, there are ways to resolve that problem and attain your goals. You must figure it out. Gary is a big promoter of garage sales and flipping things on eBay. Look for ways such as these if you find lack of money to be your go-to excuse. Get creative in ways to solve your problem. If you love animals, maybe start walking dogs ten hours a week for a little extra income. Don't let a ceiling hold you back.

Mark Cuban, from the hit show *Shark Tank,* in the beginning, when he started Micro Solutions but didn't have any money, he went to this company called Architectural lighting and told them he had no funds and asked them to front him 500 dollars. He promised them that the software and the company would work, and if he didn't make it work he promised to do whatever they needed to be done. (Like Tony Robbins says, "If you want to take the island, then burn your boats. With absolute commitment come to the insights that create real victory.")

That's what Mark Cuban did. He had no choice but to succeed, or basically, he would have had to do whatever the company asked. He built the company and ended up selling it down the line, but he was determined enough not to let a lack of funds stop him. At this writing, Mark Cub has a net worth of about 4.3 billion US dollars. He was bold, creative, innovative, and didn't make excuses, and he still is.

What kind of excuses are you making in your life that keeps you from attaining your goals, hopes, and dreams? Are you telling yourself that you lack the schooling needed to get where you are going?

An article by Fortune.com written in 2016 states, "About three out of 10 billionaires—29.9%—around the world did not have at least a bachelor's degree in 2015, according to a billionaire census by Wealth-X. That's 739 out of the total 2,473 billionaires."

So, do you think that you can't accomplish your dreams? Those 739 billionaires without a bachelor's degree are a perfect example of how the lack of schooling/or public education is not a valid excuse either!

Maybe the excuse that you keep telling yourself is 'I'm too old.' Well, that's a lame excuse too. An article on lifehack.org gives us the perfect example of this. It says, "What do Oprah Winfrey, J.K. Rowling, Dustin Hoffman, Harrison Ford, Tina Fey, and Sylvester Stallone have in common? None of them achieved major success until they were over 30 years of age." America emphasizes being young, but great wisdom and a greater sense of clarity is a gift of age. And experience makes you smarter and allows you to be more successful in life.

Think about this; Ray Kroc started McDonalds at 52. Sam Walton started Walmart at 44, and Henry Ford began at 40! You are nowhere near your 'sell by' date! When you are ready to expire, you will know you have fulfilled your purpose. Don't take yourself out of the game before you've reached your chance to shine!

Maybe your excuse is 'it's not the right time.' Just a heads up for you, it will rarely be the right time! If you wait for the right time, you are never going to start! Stop letting the notion of everything-has-to-be-perfect, the-stars-and-moon-have-to-align hold you back. Because it is holding you back and keeping you from fulfilling your true destiny!

Excuses are something that we use so we can reason our way out of why we aren't accomplishing our goals and dreams. We know that deep down, that reason is us, but we put on an act, I think because we feel ashamed or guilty of our lack of action towards our set goals. Don't let excuses control your life and keep you from reaching your dreams.

Ask Why They Said, "No"

"As I look back on my life, I realize that every time I thought I was being rejected from something good, I was actually being redirected to something better." - Steve Maraboli

When people say no to you, don't worry; opportunity or person is not meant for you. It doesn't mean that you are not worthy. It doesn't mean that you are defective. It might mean that you have more work to do. You might need to learn a new skill or go inward and work on underlying internal problems that might be holding you back. It might mean that you are worthy of the person, thing, or opportunity right for you, but the timing isn't. Never let a "no" get you down! Most people have to say "no" seven times before they can say yes!

On the way to achieving your hopes and dreams, odds are that the word "no" will be thrown in your face many times. But think about this, if it were easy, everyone would do it!

Colonel Sanders was flat broke many times in his life. At the age of sixty-two, he drove from town to town, meanwhile sleeping in his car, trying to sell his chicken recipe and get a commission. After finding someone to sell to, over a handshake, he started to gain success. He was 62! Most people want to give up so early in their lives when they have only just begun, and that's just not going to cut it if you're going to achieve your goals and dreams! You must persist even when people turn you down!

I sell Mary Kay and used to work in marketing, and we always used to say that a "no" is a "not yet." We can change and adapt and do whatever we set our minds to! We are powerful beyond measure!

So next time that person turns you down for a date, don't take it to heart. Odds are there is someone out there who is more well suited for you and your dreams out there just waiting for you! They are waiting to treat you like the king or queen you are! Next, time a job or an internship tells you "no", know that maybe that job isn't meant for you, it means perhaps *try-harder-stupid,* or perhaps it means not yet.

When I was in marketing, my job was to book 20 to 40 interviews each day to come in and interview the next day. I had to make 100 to 160 calls a day, but I hit the mark most of the time. I even started recruiting for an office out of state! So, not only was I responsible for those 20 to 40 interviews, I was responsible for 10 to 12 more. The day can be long when you are cold calling people who don't want a job in marketing, hang up the phone on you and tell you "no" But that's what I had to do. That was my job. When I worked that job, I heard "no" all the time.

Jack Canfield, *Chicken Soup for the Soul* author and author of *The Success Principles,* says to become an "askhole." Haha, I like that one.

Howard Schultz was turned down 217 times by banks and investors. If he had taken that as an answer, there would be no Starbucks. Then where would my brother, Andrew get his Mocha Frappuccino?

Bruce Springsteen was told by countless people that his voice wasn't fit for popular music and that he should just shut up and play the guitar. But if he had done that, we would have never been graced with his hit, *Born in the USA,* along with countless others.

One story of someone who overcame tremendous adversity and countless "no's" is the story of *Rocky* and Sylvester Stallone.

He was married, and they hardly had any money. His wife, at the time, begged him to get a job, but he knew if he got a regular job, he would become complacent. His whole life, he knew that he wanted to be in the movies, and he wanted to inspire people. But during the process of becoming who we now know him as he attests to being thrown out of agencies in New York at least fifteen hundred times. And not because there were that many but because he kept going back, and he kept trying.

Stallone had played minor roles in a few movies that weren't heavy hitters but continued to press on and was often faced with rejection. He was hungry and couldn't afford heat in his and his wife's apartment. One day, he went to the library (because his apartment was so cold), and found this book on Edgar Allan Poe.

Poe inspired him to stop thinking of himself so much and made him want to be of more service to others. It was at this point of his life that Stallone decided to become a writer. So, he wrote several scripts but had little luck. Finally, with only fifty dollars in his pocket, he sold a script called *Paradise Alley*. (He ended up making the movie years later but at that point in time he sold it for $100.00.)

Time passed, and he became so desperate that he sold his wife's jewelry. He said that was basically the end of their relationship. But the thing that Stallone loved most in the world was his dog. He fell on such hard times that he went down to the liquor store, stood on the corner, and tried to sell his dog. (This is what makes me the saddest.) He tried to sell his dog to strangers for fifty bucks. However, a man came up and negotiated him down to twenty-five dollars. He walked away from selling the dog to the man crying and admitted that it was one of the worst days of his life.

Two weeks later, he found himself watching a fight between Muhammad Ali and Chuck Wepner. He became inspired. When the fight ended, Stallone started writing and didn't stop for twenty straight hours. He didn't even stop to sleep. And when he had finished, he had the whole story of *Rocky* written.

He wrote down all the negative criticisms of his movie that he had heard while making the film come to life, and he read those aloud the night of the Oscars when they won!

But before the success, he had a tough time getting people on board. Finally, he had some people that read the script and loved it. They made Stallone an offer. They offered him $125,000.00 for his script. And he turned them down. Want to know why? Because they said, he couldn't star in it like he dreamed of doing. He tried to tell the people that he was Rocky, and this was his movie. But they said to him that they weren't going to put a "nobody" in the leading role.

A few weeks later, they called Stallone back and offered him a quarter of a million dollars not to star in his movie. Again, he turned it down. They raised their offer, offering him $325,000.00 not to star in his film, but he still wouldn't take it. In the end, they made him a deal and said that if he insisted on staring in it, they weren't going to put a lot of money into it and would give him $35,000.00. He accepted this final offer.

The first thing he did was he went to that same liquor store, where he sold his dog for twenty-five dollars and waited three days until the man who bought the dog arrived again. Stallone expressed to the man how much he loved the dog and didn't want to sell him in the first place. He told the man he wanted to buy back his dog. And the man said, no way! He offered the man one hundred dollars to repurchase his dog, and the man refused. Stallone upped his offer. Five hundred dollars for his dog, he offered. The man refused. He said, one thousand dollars for my dog. The man had Stallone's dog for about a month and a half at this point and had begun to take a liking to the dog. Again, he refused.

In the end, Stallone got his dog back for the price of $15,000.00 and a part in *Rocky*. This story is an excellent example of someone overcoming obstacles, believing in themselves, and not taking "no" for an answer. If Sylvester Stallone had taken "no" for an answer, he would have never been a writer or actor. *Rocky* may have been a dream that never became a reality, and he might not have ever gotten his beloved dog back. Sylvester is an excellent example of someone who knew exactly what they wanted and wouldn't stop until they achieved what they intended!

You can be just like Stallone! You have the capacity, grit, smarts, passion, and perseverance to make it to wherever you are going! You can do anything that you set your mind to! Now, will it be easy? Probably not. Will success be a straight line? No. Will it be worth it? Most certainly!

"No" is just another word in the English language. Don't let it have so much power over you. And if you are going to let it have power over you, pretend you are Webster and give it another meaning! I would also highly recommend eliminating it from your vocabulary. ☺

Read – It's Where It's At

"Not all readers are leaders, but all leaders are readers." - Harry Truman

It's no secret that the people who get ahead in life are perpetual learners. The ones who are always seeking to expand their knowledge base, learn new skills, and apply what they learned. Many successful people have rich libraries and spend hours of their day reading!

They spend time reading to help manifest their hopes and dreams rather than spending most of their time putting money in other people's wallets. It doesn't make sense for you not to! You have 24 hours in a day! Don't tell me you don't have time to devote to reading! To commit yourself to expanding your mind and your skill set.

Warren Buffett reads 5 to 6 hours a day. Around the age of 11, he had read almost all the books on wealth building in the Omaha Nebraska Library. And you think this is a coincidence when it comes to his massive success? I think not. His friend Bill Gates reads about 50 books a year (a little less than one a week). Mark Cuban reads 3 hours a day. Elon Musk read up to 10 hours a day before being a co-founder and CEO. Mind you, he read a lot of science fiction, perhaps that aided in his creative abilities. But I would say the others are reading a lot of nonfiction.

Oprah is an avid reader. And if somehow you have been living under a rock and that is news to you, check out Oprah's Book Club and books that she has authored and others that she recommends. Usually, if it has Oprah's stamp of approval, it's damn good!

Tony Robbins has said that he took it upon himself at an early age to read and learn as much as he could. He read approximately 700 books in 7 years! That's more than one book a week! Almost two books per week!

Most CEOs are said to read about one book a week resulting in 52 books per year. Some high achievers read a book a day.

My goal in 2020 is to read at least 52 books this year, and I'm already averaging more than four books a month.

Find a way that works for you, and be sure that you consume this knowledge at a high volume. We can learn so much from the people who have come before us. Almost every book I read, I find that I learn at least one key thing that changes my typical day to day life for the better. Reading is amazing.

Suze Orman has said that if you can't afford to buy her books, she encourages you to go to your local library and check it out. Why is she saying this? Because she knows that the knowledge from her books and the books of others has the power to transform your life. And she wants to transform yours. At thirty years of age, she was still a waitress making $400.00 a month, and just look at her now. If she can do it, I know that you can do it too!

Take some of the time that you usually spend scrolling through your social media, liking and hearting pictures and posts, and pick up a book! Start downloading information!

"There are so many people who have lived and died before you. You will never have a new problem. You're not ever going to have a new problem. Somebody wrote the answer down in a book somewhere." -Will Smith

I love this quote by Will Smith. I have always wanted to write a song about the fact that there are no new problems. It's true. Don't think that what you are going through has not been experienced, felt, and overcome by someone who has come before you because it has. Seek the solution to your dilemma, and you will find it. I promise.

"When I want to discover something, I begin by reading up everything that has been done along that line in the past, that's what all the books in the library are for." -Thomas Edison

If you think libraries are old or outdated, you are wrong, very wrong. They are such a fantastic source for you to gain knowledge and wisdom. They are a fantastic resource for studying the topics that interest you or the profession you work in. By reading books, you can learn from the mistakes and successes of others. Perhaps, you can spend a little less time making the same mistakes and have some more wins.

"From a child, I was fond of reading, and all the little money that came into my hands was ever laid out in books." -Benjamin Franklin

Perhaps, you find yourself struggling with your finances and can't seem to get ahead. Instead of not having enough money at the end of your month, try reading books by Patrice C. Washington, David Bach, Suze Orman, Dave Ramsey, and other financial experts who know what they are talking about. Odds are the reason for your struggles have been exposed in the pages of their books, and the answers to your troubles are there, as well.

"Once you learn to read, you will be forever free. Knowledge makes a man unfit to be a slave." -Frederick Douglas

I think we have a modern version of imprisonment because most people go to work and must do as their boss says, they can't afford to quit or have an opinion. Because nearly half of the American population or more are living paycheck to paycheck, I think that knowledge could be their ticket out of that vicious cycle that some of us know all too well.

Some people are thankful in hindsight for time in prison because they claim that reading transformed them. Resulting in a significant shift in their mind, perspective and lives when they finally found themselves released from prison. Some people in prison have found themselves reading for up to 15 hours a day or more. Imagine how much you could learn given that time!

"To spend 30 dollars to get one idea that can help propel me and make my businesses better, it was a bargain. I'll read hours every day because all it takes is one little thing to propel you to the next level." -Mark Cuban

Now, if Mark Cuban isn't a good example of a leader who is a reader, I don't know who is. He is a very successful businessman (often seen on the show *Shark Tank*. By the way, Mark, if you're reading this, my parents and I love the show.) Mark knows the importance of reading and reading daily and how it can change your life.

"I really had a lot of dreams when I was a kid, and I think a great deal of that grew out of the fact that I had a chance to read a lot." -Bill Gates

That's another thing that I love about reading! Sometimes, when people lack dreams or ambition, it is not because they are lazy or unwanting. Sometimes, it is because they simply do not know what is possible for their life! When you can read about what other people have accomplished, what they intend to do, the type of relationships they have, the environment in which they live, and the material possessions they own, you're thinking about what is possible for you and your life begins to change! A whole world opens up, and people start dreaming bigger and going after goals that they never thought were possible.

Tai Lopez talks about reading a book a day. He even gave a TEDx Talk about it in 2015. He says that successful people such as Bill Gates, Warren Buffet, the Dali Lama, Mother Teresa, and more don't have to be these sought-after mentors that we never gain once ounce of wisdom from. We can gain the knowledge and understanding that they offer through books written by them or about them. We can begin to learn their strategies for success and from their mistakes.

One of his mentors asked Tai to think back on what he wanted to be when he was sixteen. He said that is the truest version of yourself. The problem with a lot of people today, especially in America, is that we all want a good life, but we don't all get it, and I think that is partially because people don't do what is necessary to have it but also because people don't even know what to do. That is where the knowledge and wisdom comes from. Making reading one of your daily habits is crucial.

Tai Lopez wrote his grandfather a letter when he was younger asking him to help him design his dream life. What he learned from writing the letter to his grandfather and through his grandfather's response was that you will not find all the answers you seek from one person. That is why you must often read and vary the authors that you read.

His grandfather sent him a package of 11 books out of his vast library. Tai then learned by reading, you can download the mindset of the smartest, wisest, most intelligent, and the most experienced people that came before you. And there it is all laid out before you in black and white, for you to soak up and learn.

Lopez would take notes on notecards as he read and would call them "Mental Shortcuts." Then he started to travel and went to 51 countries. When he read a book, he would feel compelled to speak to the author or the person the book was about.

He decided to focus his travels and his readings on two things: health and happiness. Because of this, he didn't pay enough attention to his finances and eventually ran out of money. Tai phoned his mother to ask her if it was okay if he stayed with her until he got back on his feet, and his mother said yes. So, he returned to North Carolina to briefly stay with his mother.

Sleeping on his mother's couch, he tried to analyze where he went wrong in trying to find the good life. He had no college education and didn't know what to do. He had remembered that his grandfather told him to look outward instead of inward. Tai reached, and his uncle said that he needed to find someone to teach him how to build his fortune. Now, all he had to do was find this person.

After going to the kitchen and flipping through the yellow pages (for all you young-ins out there who don't know what yellow pages are…feel free to google them now or ask an older adult) he found a man who appeared to be a finance expert and may have been able to help. He put on the only suit that he could find and decided to visit the man.

Tai offered to work for the man for free if he would only show him what he knew. The man mentioned that he had been looking for someone like Tai for approximately 20 years and told him to come back in the morning. The man was one of his first mentors. He is now an entrepreneur, an investor, a consultant, and a partner to plenty of businesses.

Reading a book, a day, and having his book club are just two things that Tai boasts about these days. Read. Seek knowledge. Seek out mentors who are willing to help you get to where you are going.

"Your ability to copy is the biggest predictor of the success you will have in life." – Tai Lopez

"Good artists copy, great artists steal." – Pablo Picasso

I can tell you that I can personally relate to the Picasso quote when it comes to music. Don't get me wrong, I write my own songs. Still, I love copying little things that greats like Ella Fitzgerald and Amy Winehouse used to do and inputting them in jazz standards that I sing today or even some of the vocal stylings I do with my original tunes. That is very true.

Tai Lopez particularly admires Sam Walton, who started Walmart and became a massive success. He talks of this trip to Sao Paulo, Brazil, that Sam took. While Sam was there, he lived with a host family. His host family received a call one day to bail Mr. Walton out of jail. The host family asked the police if they were crazy and demanded to know why they arrested him. The police said that they found him crawling around the floors of stores.

What Mr. Walton was doing was taking a tape measure to measure how wide the aisles were in case; the Brazilians knew something that he didn't know. What a fantastic story of humility!

Sam Walton was doing this when he was already a billionaire!

"If we encounter a man of rare intellect, we should ask him what books he reads." -Ralph Waldo Emerson

"Reading is important. If you know how to read, then the whole world opens up to you." - President Barack Obama

So, you get my point. Your life can change dramatically if you limit your time on items, activities, and people who aren't helping you grow and become your highest self. Spend more time reading and developing new ideas. Learning from what someone else did well and not so well.

You will then be able to hold more intelligent conversations, and people will be intrigued and want to conversate with you more often. For those of you who are single, it will make you more appealing to the opposite sex, leaving you will more material and topics to discuss on a first date than just asking questions like, *how many brothers and sisters do you have?* When you read, you are also more empathetic and understand what people are going through and their motivations. Thus, in the process, you may become a kinder individual.

Also, every book in your local library is entirely free to read and check out and check out again. Why not take advantage of that? You must be crazy not to! And they have computers for everyone to use as well. Right there is so much access to FREE information that you would be out of your mind not to take advantage of it.

Please note that if you can speed up your learning beyond that of your peers, good things will manifest. Reading exposes you to many new thoughts, lessons, ideas, and words of wisdom. So, I suggest changing some of your "Netflix and chill" time to reading, growing, and developing your mind. You will never regret investing in yourself. It is essential.

It's All in Your Head

"Whatever the mind can conceive and believe the mind can achieve." - Napoleon Hill

Just think that there are people who prosper in recessions and depressions. Why do you think that is? During these times, most people are hurting financially. But some are thriving. Why is that?

You may hear people say that these people are greedy and capitalize off of people's misfortune. For a small percentage of people, that may be true, I wouldn't know for sure. But most of these people have a different mindset than you. These people see the economic downfall as an opportunity and not as a problem.

They look for gaps in the goods and services being provided and try to find a way to serve people better. They look for ways to eliminate suffering and invent a good or service to make people's lives easier. They think along the lines of *'What can I do to help?'* instead of *'Why is this happening to me?'* So, look at the role you are playing in your current situation and whether your recent story is helping you or hurting you.

"The mind is everything. What you think, you become." -Buddha

If you think that you have the power to accomplish your hopes, goals, and dreams, despite what anyone else tells you, odds are you will. If you think that you don't stand a fighting chance and you might as well give up now, odds are you're right. Our brains and bodies help us execute our thoughts. Our habits are often a product of our beliefs. Sometimes we find it hard to change our habits because we haven't changed our beliefs. Beliefs are usually handed down from generation to generation. Some women have a belief that says all the good men are gay or taken. And how do you think that affects the men they attract to them? It has a dramatic impact. Just know that the generational beliefs that no longer serve you can be changed. It can end with you.

You also get to *decide* whether you live in a *friendly or hostile universe*. This decision alone will be a significant determining factor in the outcome of your life. You can choose to believe that you are safe and divinely protected, or you can choose to believe that people are after you as soon as you walk out your door. And as you read/listen to that sentence, notice the emotions that rise up with both of those options. For me, being safe and divinely protected makes me smile, feel at ease, and feel the warm sun on my face. The hostile option where people are constantly trying to come after you makes me want to shrink, curl up in a ball, and never leave my house. Now, which one of those beliefs about the universe do you think will attract better? And which one do you think will have you encounter more crime, anger, sadness, and feeling of being a victim? Which of these, the friendly or the hostile universe, do you think is the best for promoting overall health or healthy relationships? It's simple. We all write our own stories, and it's time for you to focus on what you are writing.

"The mind is a wonderful servant, but a terrible master." — Robin Sharma

Dr. Joe Dispenza said one day he met his friend who was a millionaire for lunch, and he said that his friend said, "Today I lost everything that I owned, pass the ketchup." He did as his friend asked and said to his friend, "Jerry, aren't you upset?" He asked Joe what he meant, and he clarified, "well, you lost everything, you know, you owned." Dr. Dispenza said his friend Jerry then looked at him and said, "I am money. I've made it thousands of times. I've made it a hundred times, so I am going to make it back in two weeks."

When I heard this, I was in awe. It amazes me that some people's mindset is different and their difference in mentality causes them to do such amazing things. They reach heights that none had ever dreamt of before. Most people who lost a million dollars would call it quits and sulk. Not this friend of Joe's. It just shows that all the power is in your mind and what happens to you in this life is up to you. You can choose to react in defeat, or you can choose to respond with a specific determination because you know deep down that you are indeed the creator of your life. No one else gets to set the scene. You are the painter of your life. You get to make the decision, and you get to decide how your story reads.

In an interview called, *The Power of Consciousness*, Dr. Bruce Lipton says, "You have 50 trillion cells living in community, but your mind is the government. When a government works in harmony with the people, then the people thrive, and the community is in good health and grows. But when a government is not supportive or not working in harmony with a community, then the government can cause the nature of that community to fall apart or even lead to the end of the community." Our minds, like he said, are the government of these cells, and when we live in harmony and focus on the good and feed the mind good things, we can thrive. But If we are not doing that, we can cause illness in our bodies and manifest things that don't align with the life that we say we want.

To have harmony between your body and mind, eat good foods, reduce or eliminate stress, live in a positive environment, etc. You must do these things and more to keep your mind so that it can aid you in living your best life possible.

In that same interview, he explains it in further detail, "And the answer is, my thoughts influence my brain, and the brain releases chemistry that matches my thoughts." Therefore, we have to be so careful. The thoughts you are thinking will determine your reality. They will manifest in your life. Again, you are the creator of your own reality. Do not let your thoughts go in a negative downward spiral, no matter what your situation is. Focus instead on what you would like to manifest and who you would like to become.

The following is one thing that Les Brown has memorized and will recite in his speeches.

"I do not choose to be man,

It is my right to be uncommon ... if I can,

I seek opportunity ... not security.

I do not wish to be a kept citizen.

Humbled and dulled by having the

State looks after me.

I want to take the calculated risk;

To dream and to build.

To fail and to succeed.

I refuse to live from hand to mouth;

I prefer the challenges of life

To the guaranteed existence;

The thrill of fulfillment

To the stale calm of Utopia.

I will never cower before any master

Nor bend to any threat.

It is my heritage to stand erect.

Proud and unafraid;

to face the world boldly and say:

This, I have done."

The people who succeed in this life are the ones who do what others don't. They think differently. They have daily habits that aid them in their success and don't hinder them. They see things before they come to pass. They focus on gratitude and they don't let their mind win!

Mastering your mind and controlling your thoughts and emotions is hard but it can be done. Don't give in to your mind. Your mind is focused on keeping you continuing down the path of familiarity. Your mind doesn't want you to take risks because it isn't safe. Your mind is designed to keep you alive. But it can be used as a tool for good. It can work in your favor, or it can work against you. The decision is yours.

Take Care of Your Body

"Take care of your body. It's the only place you have to live." -Jim Rohn

If you didn't know, it is so important to take vitamin C and vitamin D and make sure you are getting aligned by a good chiropractor. The alignment of your spine helps for better overall nervous system function, and vitamin C boosts your immune system, increasing your white blood cell count. And all this is very important for overall health and to fight off illnesses. Make sure you are drinking green tea and lots of water. Sometimes the simple things are the best.

Make sure; if you are an adult, you are getting at least 20 minutes of daily exercise for overall health. For weight loss, I would increase the amount of time. I would advise finding something that gets you moving that you like to do. You can swim, bike, walk, run, practice yoga, lift weights, practice martial arts, dance, or get on the stair stepper. Whatever it is, I just want you to get up and get moving.

I love cardio (almost to a fault), so you never have to motivate me to go for a run, walk, or swim. But I need the motivation to do my weight training (even though I always feel so powerful afterward). And as much as I wouldn't like it to be the case, you need both. You need both cardio and strength training for optimum health. I would be careful when you start, especially if you haven't exercised in a while, take it slow and just do what you can, even if it's only walking around the block. Don't go from zero to hero right away. Work your way up by setting goals for your daily workouts and accomplish a little more each day.

Don't forget to talk to your doctor. Diet and exercise are two things that trip people up. We know if we eat healthily and get a decent amount of exercise, we will be in good standing, but many times, we fail to do so. So, always talk to your doctor before you go too hard in the paint and make sure what you want to put in place in your life when it comes to diet and exercise, is suitable for you, your environment, and your body.

Being in excellent health will help you stand taller, be more confident, and have more energy. Believe me; if you are doing it right, you will be amazed at the power that shows up that you never knew you had.

Don't buy into these weight loss pills and all the bull they try to sell you on television. We all know how to eat clean and exercise. It's not about being any particular size. It's about being the healthiest you that you can be, for your God, your family, and your work. Take care of the house your soul lives in and treat it like a mansion made of gold!

Spend time with your friends. Spending time with your friends is a great way to reduce your stress levels. Sharing a smile and laugh is healing. Perhaps, you just moved to a new area or have difficulty making friends because you are shy. If that is the case, join a club, volunteer group, or another type of organization.

Another crucial thing is doing something that you love AT LEAST once a day. If you can do something that you love more than once a day, that's great, but make sure you do that at least once a day. For instance, I like to read. I read motivational books, religious books, autobiographies, books about money, psychology, business, or music. Reading this kind of material inspires me and educates me. I make goals to read daily, weekly, monthly, and yearly because it's important to me. Perhaps you like to paint! Don't deprive yourself of the privilege. Maybe you want to work in your garden. One of my best friends loves to garden, and you can often find her working on her flower beds and her garden. It gives her peace. Gardening relaxes her mind and allows her to destress.

Take time to relax. I know people who love to take baths. If they can draw a bath, they are happy campers! They need to take time to wind down and relax. For some people (including myself), long walks in nature are one of the most relaxing things you can do. For me, it exercises my body, and at the same time, I get to witness life, gaze at the beauty of the world, which makes me thankful and allows me to slow down and get away from all the distractions of the world. Perhaps, you need to go in and get a massage. Proper alignment of your back and the release of tensions in your body will do wonders for your overall health. You may not even know it, but you may be carrying your problems around with you.

Meditation is so powerful. It's a great way to listen for direction from our higher power and a great way to slow down. To take our busy minds and free them from all the clutter that we fill them up with day in and day out. Meditation has been linked to positive health.

And I know this one sounds like a no-brainer but make sure you are practicing proper hygiene, washing your hair and body, brushing your teeth, and anything else that you should be doing to take care of yourself or that is part of your routine. Proper hygiene leads to longevity. Another thing about proper hygiene is when you look good, smell good, and feel good, which will make you more confident, and people, in turn, will want to be around you. When people want to be around you, you will be blessed with relationships and opportunities that can better your life, as well.

Avoid drugs and alcohol. I don't use drugs, but I can say from personal experience that I know (almost too well) the harmful effects of alcohol. Some of these effects include, forgetting what you did the night before, falling and bruising your body, waking up with a hangover, especially, a headache or vomiting, making bad decisions such as drinking and driving, or engaging in promiscuous behavior.

High achievers are not people who wake up every morning constantly trying to recover from the night before. If this is you (don't feel like I'm pointing the finger; this has been me at times, too), you need to break this cycle and break away from this damaging behavior.

You may want to be radical and cut yourself off cold turkey and never go back. Or maybe you are the type who needs to simply limit your alcohol or drug consumption. Seek professional help from a trusted therapist and seek groups such as AA if you think you need to. Don't let drugs and alcohol destroy your life internally and externally. It is never too late to make a change, and I have complete confidence that you can do whatever you set your mind to.

Eat healthy foods. That is something that I have to force myself to do. I don't gravitate towards eating vegetables. And even now, I often fall short. I must force myself to make sure I am consuming these. I must get creative with how I incorporate these into my diet. I am not good at eating as healthy as I should, but I am working on it. I can feel a difference in my body when I have a dish that may be something like fish and fruits than when I eat a greasy pizza. But like most Americans, I want to go for pizza over the healthy choice. That is where we must work on reprogramming our minds. We must create rewards for going with healthy options.

Make sure you are getting the proper sleep and exercising, and avoiding the pitfalls that so often take us down. You can be healthy. Your body wants you to take care of it and for you to treat it like a car you consider to be your prized possession. Your body is a miraculous thing. Take care of it. It's your vehicle to carry you through this life.

Your Energy

"Everything is energy and that's all there is to it. Match the frequency of the reality you want and you cannot help but get that reality. It can be no other way. This is not philosophy. This is physics." - Albert Einstein

    In quantum physics, you will hear them talk about the field. They define it as "invisible and moving energy that influences a physical world." Many define this as spirit, too. Here we see where science and spirituality meet.

    We are souls and energetic beings using our physical bodies as a house, and when we realize this, we begin to focus more on where our energy is going and the power that we are putting out. We do things like meditation or rest and relaxation (not sitting in front of your T.V.) When studying the flow of energy, we conclude that the material things don't matter as much, and we realize that the energy we are projecting towards ourselves and others is why we are attracting what we are into our lives. Want to change the things you are attracting to you? Change your energy. Are you attracting miserable people? Look at yourself? Are you miserable? Because I don't know too many happy, fun-loving people who hang out with miserable people. Are you excited about your work, or do you flirt with the clock all day? Either way, people can tell, and it affects your future raises and promotions.

Dr. Bruce Lipton says, "that the invisible stuff" (meaning energy "is more powerful than the physical stuff") meaning material things. In this book, you've heard me preach time and again about the power of our beliefs, our thoughts, and just our mind overall. And that's where many people go wrong in the journey to becoming their highest self. They just don't buy into the reality of, to change, you must change. Stop blaming your boss for passing you up on that promotion. Stop blaming your spouse for the fact that you haven't started your own business. It boils down to your thoughts, beliefs, overall energy, and the inner work, your actions.

Dr. Lipton talks of the fact that I have always believed to be true, that the world can be a completely different place than the one we live in. We can have a better world. "Let's consciously create a different world," he says. And we can do this.Marianne Williamson touched on this in her efforts to become democratic nominee for president, and everyone thought she was nuts. The thoughts of the collective are mighty people, and neither Lipton nor Williamson is lying. They are both telling the truth.

"What we're facing is an evolution, not a physical evolution. It's how we relate to each other with our consciousness. So, we're all coming together in one giant consciousness called 'Humanity.' This is the evolution we are facing." - Dr. Bruce Lipton

I think we saw some of this during the COVID-19 crisis. We came together during that time. No matter your political affiliation, race, gender, or background, we knew that no one was immune to the coronavirus, and I saw more kindness seeping out of everyone's pores. We consciously chose to treat people with a different level of kindness and compassion. And speaking for myself, I hadn't seen that in the collective in a long time.

Abraham Hicks is a great teacher of the law of attraction, and a lot of that has to do with your thoughts, beliefs, and energy. Listen to anyone of Abraham's talks, and you will know that is true.

Ever feel like you want many things to manifest in your life, and it feels like you are on a treadmill simply running in place? You are doing a lot of work to make sure your dreams start to manifest in your life but instead, you feel overworked, underappreciated, and stuck. I've been there. You are doing a lot of work externally, but you're not rewriting that negative programming, shifting your thoughts and beliefs and your energy. If you want to have high energy, do things and be around people who make you happy, motivate and energize you. Don't grab the bag of chips when you are hungry; instead, grab an apple. If you feel lethargic after eating, don't eat that food! All in all, pay attention to what fuels you and makes you feel like you are wearing a backpack with a rocket inside it that nobody can see. That imagery is fantastic because not only are you excited to be propelled to the next level, but your backpack covers the rocket so, it's a secret that only you know about. 😊

Your reality is whatever you make it to be. The world can be sunshine and rainbows for you, or it can be the jail that Batman had to climb out of in *The Dark Knight Rises*. The good news is that it's up to you. You and you alone get to choose if you live in a friendly or hostile universe. I am among the many that believe we live in a friendly universe. I think most people are good. And after listening to Louise Hay's affirmations, I believe that I am safe and divinely protected. I have decided that this is the world I live in.

Now, if you were to compare my energy to someone who believes that we live in a hostile universe, I'm confident you would see a difference. The differences may appear in the way we treat and interact with others. They may appear in our overall health, our friendships, romantic relationships, and so on. I think that just the fact that we are on planet Earth with enough oxygen to survive and thrive as we are floating around in space is a miracle in itself, and that's enough for me.

If you want an example of a couple of people with incredible and infectious energy, pay attention to Tony Robbins, Matthew McConaughey, and Pharrell Williams. The energy that these men exude is contagious. They (without verbalizing it) almost invite you to come and vibrate higher. They make you feel better than you did before. They make you want to be around them. Most of the time, they embrace life, smile, and work to better the world in some way, shape, or form. You can't help but be drawn to them. That's a great way to be.

Maya Angelou said, "I've learned that people will forget what you said, people will forget what you did, but people will never forget how you made them feel."

That's what Tony, Matthew, and Pharrell have in common. People don't always remember their every word, but I think one of the reasons for their massive success is because of their energy. You want to continue to be around them, listen to their videos/music, or watch their movies. They have a powerful platform because of the energy that they exude day in and day out.

Chakras are simply proof that we are energy. I am beginning to learn more about them, but I know for sure that they are real.

Iarp.org states, "Chakras are the concentrated energy centers of the body. Chakra is a Sanskrit term and it means "wheel" or "disk" and is derived from the root word "chakra". Chakras are spinning wheels of energy/light."

These are the major chakras: crown, third eye, throat, heart, solar plexus, sacral, and root. We have both major and minor Chakras. Depression, anxiety (and other forms of the like), unhealthy eating habits, lack of sleep, lying, and more can throw off our energy and keep us from performing and being our highest purest self.

Energy is something that is flowing and there whether we like it or not. We can shut ourselves off from the world and vibrate at a low level, or we can make an honest effort to be our best self possible and vibrate high. Again, as I have said before, it is your decision. You are in the driver's seat of your own life. If you want something different than your current reality, it is time to start taking action and start doing the things in your life that will raise your energy!

4 Minute Mile

"Doctors and scientists said breaking the four-minute mile was impossible, that one would die in the attempt. Thus, when I got up from the track after collapsing at the finish line, I figured I was dead."
-Roger Bannister

Roger Bannister, in 1954, at the age of 25, was the first to ever run a mile in four minutes or less. His time was 3:59.4. Since then, 1,400 male athletes have broken the "four-minute barrier," but it was unheard of before him. Why is this?

It is now the standard for many middle-distance runners in certain cultures. And Bannister's impressive feat has even been beaten by 17 seconds by a man named Hicham El Guerrouj of Morocco in 1999 at age 24. He has since retired but still is a world record holder of several outdoor events.

Just because something hasn't been done or they say it's impossible does not mean that it can't be done. I'm sure you have heard the saying, "The world literally says, 'I'm possible."

TD Jakes always talks about the Wright Brothers and says that they thought, *I belong up there!*

So, what I want to know is, what is your four-minute mile? What have you been longing to do? What have you wanted to achieve that has never been done before? Because just because it hasn't been done doesn't mean it can't be done. The human mind is a remarkable thing, and the human will is even stronger.

Do not let anyone else's limiting beliefs keep you from shattering glass ceilings and knocking down doors. You can do whatever it is you set your mind to. And the only person you need to believe in is yourself.

Be Curious

"There is divine beauty in learning.... To learn means to accept the postulate that life did not begin at my birth. Others have been here before me, and I walk in their footsteps." —Elie Wiesel

Earners are learners. I've heard plenty of times that *I don't like to read. Bullshit.* Yeah, and I wouldn't say I like making calls to book gigs either. But I like playing gigs, and I like the money I get from playing gigs. So, that, in turn, is part of the process. There were some days when I was writing this book where I had to force myself to sit down and write. But I wanted to be an accomplished author more than I didn't want to write.

What I am saying is, if you're not an avid reader, you better become one. But there are so many other ways to learn and gather information. There are in-person classes, online classes, there are seminars, workshops, webinars, and documentaries. There are so many ways to learn. Stop telling yourself that insane lie that you don't have the time. You have time for Pinterest, video games, television, Facebook, etc. I don't want to hear you don't have time. If you are not willing to do what needs to be done, perhaps you don't deserve the success you're longing for. Someone else will gladly put in the work.

Also, learners are curious about so many things: poetry, art, history, economics, business, medicine, marketing, psychology, astronomy, etc. They have a wide array of interests and are very passionate about learning. I don't know what to tell you if this isn't the way you are wired because I have always been this way. I am interested in so many areas of life. Things like Shakespeare all the way to the rise of the robots which will be slowly eliminating and debatably recreating jobs within the next 20 to 30 years. No one has to get on my case about reading, taking classes, or trying to learn more information about any subject.

If you aren't already like this, I would highly suggest that you get passionate about learning. If you don't, others will take advantage of educational opportunities and will learn what you wouldn't. This will help them get closer to reaching their goals.

Use What You Believe In (Religious/Spiritual) To Help You Navigate Your Journey

"When you come out of the storm, you won't be the same person that walked in. That's what this storm's all about." -Haruki Murakam

When the storms come (and they will), you will need something to cling to. I know I sound like a Debbie Downer saying that storms are inevitable but from what I've seen thus far, they are. I know it contradicts this parchment of positivity but what I am saying is that you need some kind of belief to help you navigate your way through the difficult times.

No, I'm not promoting Christianity or any other religion. And I am more than sure that I will catch some flack from people for saying this. But all I am saying is you need to believe in something. It's crucial to center who you are and communicate with the divine.

I was raised Catholic but wouldn't consider myself a Catholic now. I would say I'm more of a

Christian with an open mind, or should I say spiritual. And that works for me. It may not work for you, and that's OKAY. Find what works for you and use it to propel you to be the highest version of yourself.

One storm that tested many of us at all different levels I would say, was the 2020 COVID-19 outbreak and just when we thought it was over it lingered for the following years.. Not only did it confine us to our homes, take a significant toll on the economy, take a toll on the overall health of our nation and our world, but it also dramatically tested our beliefs. It tested our beliefs in government, in spirituality, in economy, in health, in education, in social structure, in safety, in cleanliness and so on. That was a time in my life that I found my faith in the divine deepened and intensified. It was at this point that I prayed as I had never prayed before. Not only was I praying for our overall health as a nation and as a world, I prayed for the virus to end and for things to return to normal. I prayed for the safety of my family and my friends. I prayed for the safety of all the doctors, nurses, and healthcare workers. I prayed for the protection of all the grocery store workers, gas station attendants, pharmaceutical workers, and any other "essential" workers.

I prayed for a miracle. With that said, prayer may not be right for you. Perhaps you have another method of speaking with the divine. And I am saying, do what works for you! I prayed for the healing of the world.

When times like these come and they will, you are going to need this. Some people lost their entire families in the crisis. I couldn't even begin to imagine. And I'm sure if any human has ever been through something similar, belief in something higher than yourself won't bring your family back, but it will most certainly help.

A crisis inevitably will happen; I hate to break it to you. But if we can keep a positive mental attitude and lean on spiritual beliefs and understanding, we can learn to make the most of it and come out of the crisis improved.

While researching this book, I came across some wise words on the benefits of a crisis from Dr. Myles Munroe on crisis. They are as follows:

"Crisis is the incubator of creativity."

"Crisis demands a new way of thinking about old problems."

"Crisis is an opportunity to improve and advance over old ideas."

"Crisis produces growth and development."

"Crisis creates opportunity."

He spoke that every progressive invention that we have was birthed because there was a problem that we needed to solve. And that is so true. I think this was proven to the American people during the Covid-19 crisis. We saw genuinely remarkable things come out of such a devastating time. He also said:

"Crisis produces and manifests true leadership ability."

"Crisis ignites the passion of vision."

During times of crisis, we remember our true visions and dreams. Times of trouble help us re-center and expose what is important to us. Times of crisis strip us and allow everything that is not truly important to "fall off."

Everyone, like I said, will experience these times. And when things are going wrong, it's not time to look at your creator and say, "why me?" It's time to ask, *what can I learn from this? How can I serve others that are less fortunate than myself?*

It's essential to have some spiritual foundation to cling to otherwise the normal confusion and frustration that come with times of crises, may become unbearable.

William Shakespeare said, "Sweet are the uses of adversity."

That is a time for you to get creative and look for solutions instead of focusing on the problem. This time of crisis/ this storm was given to you to stretch you to become a better version of yourself. You, in the end, will surprise yourself and become stronger than you ever thought you could be.

"If there is a silver lining to bad times, it is this: when facing severe challenges, your mind is normally at its sharpest." -Jon Huntsman

"Humans seldom have created anything of lasting value unless they were tried or hurting" -Jon Huntsman

Take these snippets of wisdom from Mr. Huntsman and use them to your advantage!

Often when I think of someone who used a difficult time of her life and turned it around to make something incredible, I think of Adele. Before Adele made her album *21*, it is evident (if you listen to it) that she had undergone a very trying and challenging time in her personal life. But she took that pain and turned it into beautiful music, and that beautiful music resonated with so many people and made Adele a household name. Could you imagine what her life would be like if she had just sat around feeling sorry for herself?

Daily Gratitude Lists

"Gratitude turns what we have into enough, and more. It turns denial into acceptance, chaos into order, confusion into clarity...it makes sense of our past, brings peace for today, and creates a vision for tomorrow." - Melody Beattie

Oprah is a big advocate for daily gratitude lists, as am I. Every day at 10 am, I take some time to write down all the things that I am grateful for. I started with five things. And now I can fill the page of whatever it is I'm writing on. If you are not making a daily gratitude list I would highly suggest that you do so. That is a great way to shift your focus off of the problems of the world (there are many) to how blessed we are. And a vast majority of us take for granted what others would only dream of.

I'll just share with you some of the things I am grateful for (in no particular order) to show you how blessed you are and how much you take for granted. I am thankful for my family, my friends, the air in my lungs, the blood in my veins, my limbs, all of my organs working in perfect harmony, for the house I live in, for running water, electricity, my clothes, my job/s, my paycheck, the money in my bank, my cats, the written word, books, audio books, technology, the internet, YouTube,

Facebook, Instagram, videos, pictures, nature, birds, horses, music, jazz music, education, teachers, mentors and the list goes on and on!

It attracts more things to be grateful for to you. When you appreciate the things you have, you become aware of more and more things to be thankful for. Everyone has something to be thankful for, even if that is the divine waking us up again this morning. Another day on planet Earth is a gift within itself. Doing this helps to retrain your mind. It redirects your focus from all the things that are going wrong to all the things that are fabulous and that you should be shouting, "Thank you! Thank you! Thank you!" for.

"Gratitude turns what we have into enough."
– Anonymous.

Especially as Americans, we can be so caught up with greed that we spend every penny we have and more trying to buy things and accumulate material goods to impress society. We are constantly focusing on what we don't have and how what we have isn't enough. We think that once we get the promotion, the lover, or the nice house on the corner, then we can be happy. But practicing gratitude teaches us that we do have enough. And what we have been chasing are all extra blessings that we should be fine with or without. I would venture to say that many people who are middle class and above in America and possibly around the world don't understand how good we have it. We take for granted so many things like running water, a roof over our heads, electricity, and a place to sleep that others may only dream of.

One day, while scrolling through the web I found a saying, a Buddhist proverb that read, 'Enough' is a feast." I thought that was a great way to summarize in a few words, which I am trying to teach you here.

I often think about my financial situation when the tornadoes hit Nashville in March of 2020. I didn't have a lot by any means but what I did know was that I wanted to give. I wanted to help the people whose homes had been affected by the two tornadoes that swept through in the night and left my town in ruins. But as I said, I didn't have a whole lot in the bank. Nonetheless, I donated a small amount of money to a community non-profit that was collecting money for all the homes and families that had been hit and even displaced by the tornadoes. Next, I went online and found a church in Nashville that was collecting gift certificates to Home Depot, Lowes, water bottles, Gatorade, and tools. I got a small gift certificate (with what I could afford) to Lowes and dropped by that church on my way home from work.

Like I said, once you start feeling grateful and believing what you have is enough, you begin to give with no thought of receiving. And you begin to manifest a higher version of yourself. Many people in my position would say that they didn't have enough money to give. They would say things like, "It's not my fault I don't have the money to give. My employer barely pays me enough to get by." Or "Let the rich celebrities donate and give. They have plenty of money. I don't."

These are things people say when they are in lack, poverty, or victim mode. Once you start being grateful for all the amazing things you have, you start thinking of all the fantastic things that you can DO with what you have.

Hell, I am so thankful for my sight. For the ability to hear and speak. And the ability to taste great food. We take all of this for granted. "It's a funny thing about life; once you begin to take note of the things you are grateful for, you begin to lose sight of the things that you lack." -Germany Kent

I'm telling you, once you start focusing on being thankful, your whole life begins to shift. You start your journey to becoming a no-limits person. You begin to see opportunities that you didn't see before. You begin to treat your family, friends, and belongings with a different level of care, lovingness, and respect. You start waking up thankful for another day instead of cursing your alarm clock.

According to the article, "How Gratitude Rewires Your Brain And How To Make It Work

For You" by George J. Ziogas, there is evidence backed by research that gratitude can improve your overall happiness, lower stress in your body, and improve your overall health. Such a simple thing, gratitude is, but it makes a MAJOR difference in people's lives. In the article, Ziogas states, "According to UCLA's Mindfulness Awareness Research Center, regularly expressing gratitude literally changes the molecular structure of the brain, keeps the gray matter functioning, and makes us healthier and happier." This is amazing!

He talks about the importance of gratitude and how there are more significant benefits of being grateful for non-materialistic things. Parents, this is a great way to practice gratitude to be an example for your children. What cannot be sold in a store should be held higher than the material objects and wealth we acquire. It is also stated that couples who show gratitude towards one another have longer-lasting relationships and better communication than those who do not express gratitude regularly.

"The practice of gratitude increases your dopamine production, which encourages your brain to seek more of the same. It's the brain saying, "Oh, do that again", which means the more you are grateful for, the more you will find to be grateful for. Some say "what you appreciate, appreciates." On a scientific level, this is an example of Hebb's Law, which states "neurons that fire together wire together."— Carrie D. Clarke

Dopamine is a pleasure chemical produced by the brain and body and can function as a hormone or a neurotransmitter. It links to pleasure, wanting or desire, and learning. So, when you express gratitude, researchers have found, as you see above, an increase in dopamine production. That's why gratitude becomes addicting, and once you start looking for things to be grateful for consistently, you won't be able to stop.

Gratitude promotes brain activity in your hypothalamus and other parts of your brain. You feel better when you are thankful for all the things in your life that you do have instead of focusing on what's missing. That leads to desire, consumerism, hoarding, and envy, along with increased stress.

In a UC Berkeley study done in 2003, they found that if they kept a gratitude journal or focused on gratitude daily, they tested higher than people who didn't in enthusiasm, attention, energy, and determination. Because of this, they were found to have better-coping skills for when problems appeared in their lives.

Being grateful can even improve how you feel physically. It has been proven that thankfulness will help maintain healthier eating habits than not thankful for what you have. That is an excellent thing for those of us who are looking to make an overall "lifestyle change," gratitude is a great place to start. No matter how young or old or rich or poor you are, know there is always something you can be grateful for, and it is never too late to start!

In 2010, researchers at the University of Pennsylvania found that gratitude leads to a higher sense of self-worth! This is so great for all of you out there struggling and not knowing your worth, your true value! You are amazing! You are remarkable! And it has been proven that expressing gratitude can help aid you in your journey to becoming the highest version of yourself!

What I found interesting during the process of writing this book is that researchers in China found that gratitude consistently can lower rates of depression and anxiety in individuals. It also helped some sleep more soundly through the night. I know, especially in America, we have a MAJOR problem with depression and anxiety, to the point that it immobilizes people and can affect them almost every minute of the day. Knowing this, I wonder if consumerism and comparison play a role? I know there is way more to it than just being grateful, but if you can reduce anxiety and depression and improve sleep, I think it's worth making it a part of your daily routine.

Another thing about expressing gratitude for your life and what you have that is so great is that it improves our overall happiness and helps us become kinder and more compassionate. Because of this, it pours over to others. And we are nicer to everyone around us. The results of the daily practice of gratitude are astounding. Once you know the facts, you would be foolish not to make it a part of your everyday life!

If you suffer from severe stress, first, know that it is EXTREMELY UNHEALTHY! About 90% of doctor's visits are due to stress or are stress-related! It's essential to get your stress under control so you can live a very long and happy life, meanwhile sharing your gifts and talents with the world! Stress can wreck a good night's sleep, cause you to have high blood pressure, cause you to develop unhealthy habits, and cause hormonal imbalances. Believe it or not, gratitude (I know you think I'm obsessed with being grateful. Let me let you in on a little secret, I am!) can help reduce stress in the body and brain. A study done in 2007 showed that after one week of focusing on gratitude, participants showed a drop in their blood pressure and cortisol levels. They also saw an increase in heart health! Let me tell you a fantastic way to not pay as much in doctor's bills. All the cool kids are doing it, BE GRATEFUL EVERY DAY!

Dr. Joe Dispenza says that, "We can measure when a person feels gratitude for what happens to their heart. The heart gets regulated. It starts beating more coherently. It starts increasing energy to the brain. It starts creating an ambient field around the body. That is when your heart starts working for you."

When you feel gratitude, and gratitude is essential to practice even when you are not directly receiving something, you change your destiny. You are literally changing the way that your brain and your body function!. Even in the tough times we go through, there is always something that we can be grateful for!

I heard once that when you appreciate something, it appreciates! You get more in return for being grateful. I think as a society, we just take so much for granted. We forget to be thankful to have land to live on, water to drink, air to breathe, and people to love. There are many things that we think will always be there, so we don't give them the gratitude they deserve. Remember not to take the little things in life for granted. Some people aren't as lucky.

In a study, Dr. Dispenza found that if people traded their negative emotions ten minutes a day for gratitude, their immune systems improved by 50%! That's crazy! He claims that your unconscious mind does not know the difference between a real experience and the thoughts you are creating alone! Isn't that amazing. I've heard this idea reinforced and repeated by several great thinkers of our time! Our nervous system is one of the best medicines out there! We need to take advantage of what we have!

Your life will change, and it will change dramatically more and more in correlation to the amount of gratitude that you are feeling! Feel gratitude before anything happens to you. It helps you get ahead of your day and makes it harder for those old programs and old negative emotions to creep back in. As I type, alone in my quiet apartment, I am so happy and grateful that I am here now, with the clarity to think and put down on paper what I have learned and come to experience. I know that gratitude works because even on the days that I don't feel like it, I do it, and I get this rush, and it shifts my perspective.

Today, I am grateful for a lot of things: the birds that sing daily outside of my sliding glass door, the cup of hot tea on the table, the fact that I was lucky enough to receive a college education, my clothes, my phone, my computer and the chair I am sitting in. And if you want me to go on longer, I will!

The stronger the emotions we feel towards a problem the more of our power we give away, says Dr. Joe Dispenza. That's creative energy, he says, that could be directed towards creating our future. And instead of it going towards building a future that we desire, we are focusing our creative energy on the problem that has presented itself in our lives. This is where a lot of people get caught up.

It's essential to live in the present moment and break our old negative habits. We can gain control over our mind and body. Do not let it control you. It makes a terrible master but a great servant. You must remember this. You can train your body and mind to perform in a way that pleases you and aids you in living your best life!

Dr. Wayne Dyer would always remind us that we are spiritual beings having a human experience, not the other way around. That is important too. If we can remember this we can control the animal nature that is inside of us, that at times tries to take over.

You can create the life of your dreams! Stop living in the past and as a victim to your habits. Start yourself on a journey of a new way of experiencing life! Believe in the possibilities for your life!

Make It Your Signature

"Every thought you produce, anything you say, any action you do, it bears your signature." -Nhat Hanh

Denise Duffield Thomas has a book called *Get Rich, Lucky Bitch*. Among the many tips and tricks I've adopted from the book was the proclamation of who I had yet to become under my name in my signature.

Many people who sent me emails probably thought I was off my rocker. Under my name at the bottom of my emails, I had typed "Grammy Award Winning Singer/Songwriter." I am sure some people may have googled me to check and see if that was true, and some probably already knew it wasn't. But I think it forced my brain, by seeing it over and over again under my name, to define myself in a way I never had before. I was defining myself by a desired future rather than a rejected past.

Along with that, I also took to writing my goals and aspirations out on paper twice daily. The key is to write them in the present tense and to do so twice a day. Some people do it first thing when they wake up and make it the last thing they do before going to bed. I would imagine that would be more effective than the time of day in which I write mine.

If you can make it the first and last thing you do, I think that would be better. But I do what works for me. I have programmed my phone to remind me to write my goals out in the present tense at 10 am and 3 pm each day. And if I am busy when the reminder pops up, I snooze it and make sure I take time to do it every day. It's become a daily ritual. Most people who know me will attest to me doing this. When I was a server, I'd be on the line, writing my goals and aspirations in the present tense on a guest check.

    I also made a pact to myself that I wasn't going to stay a server forever. Please, let me clarify this here. I am NOT knocking anyone in the service industry. I know how hard your job is. I know how much skill and talent it takes to be good, and I know that every clog in the wheel is ESSENTIAL to our country and world to function at its highest potential. But with that being said, I knew I didn't want to stay a server forever. I knew that I wanted to do more, whether it was to own my own jazz club or café or whatever it may be. My soul longed for more. Writing my goals and aspirations every day reminded me that my situation was only temporary, and it reminded me that I could become whoever I wanted to be. I could mold myself into whomever I wanted, sort of like throwing pots.

    Some people write their goals on an index card and carry it with them. I tried this. I had several index cards with my goals and aspirations on them. I had one in my purse, one on my work desk, and one at my home just above the kitchen sink. I would take them out and look at them and read them over and over again in my head (if at work or in public). At home, I would read them out loud. I no longer have the one in my purse unless you count the list I write every day. I can't stress enough how vital the repetition of this is. And you do have to believe in it, even when you don't see how it could be at all possible.

I was always told not to attempt to understand how it would happen but always to have faith that it would happen. To be foolish in my belief, as a child. And sometimes, not worrying about the "how" of it lifts a lot of weight off of your shoulders. I am not saying, don't have a plan because I don't necessarily believe that. That's good. But I think it is crucial that you cannot unravel if your project does not unfold as you expected it to. You have to be flexible enough to know that things will come up. Doors that you thought would be open will close in your face. People who said they would always be there may not be. Things that you thought were for you may not be. The career you chose may not be the career you end up in. That's okay.

"For my thoughts are not your thoughts, neither are your ways my ways, saith the Lord" (Isaiah 55:8). Remember this. When things go wrong, and you feel like giving up. It may simply be life trying to redirect you. So, plan and believe foolishly like a child. Remind yourself of the person you are becoming and molding into. And work at it. But don't be worried about every little detail. I promise you, if you are patient, persistent, and persevere, you will achieve success and a life that you can be proud of.

Don't forget to do the small daily tasks that ordinary people don't. You are extraordinary, and you are on your way to becoming the person you wanted to be. Take the necessary actions daily, and you will be well on your way.

It's Never Too Late

"You are never too old to set another goal or to dream a new dream." – C.S. Lewis

A friend of mine gave me an intentions and reflections book to write in daily and hold myself accountable for achieving my goals and dreams. On every page of this book was the quote by C.S. Lewis that you read above. Every day it was a reminder to me that I am not a gallon of milk. It's never too late. I can be whatever I set out to be, and I don't have to feel as if I'm never going to make it or that I should give up because I have plenty of time to do what I am meant to do. My mission and life's work won't pass me by if I am actively working on myself and taking the necessary steps.

One day I came across a picture on Facebook and immediately shared it to my Timeline. In big black bold letters, the top line of the picture read, "It's never too late." The rest of the image was divided into four different quadrants, and it had a picture of Ray Kroc, who started McDonald's at age 52. Henry Ford, who began Ford Motor Company at age 40, Colonel Sanders, who started KFC at age 65, and Sam Walton, who started Walmart at age 44. That flooded my heart with joy!

So many of you out there believe that you are past your "sell by" date! I don't believe that at all! You can do anything you set your mind to! And age is nothing but a number!

Look at J-Lo and how she celebrated her 50th birthday by going on tour to perform for all her adoring fans! She is in great shape, physically and mentally, and she does not let her age define her! It even seems as if she is just warming up!

Don't let anyone tell you that you are too old to have the dreams, goals, and desires that you hold in your heart! Take the necessary actions to train your body and mind and let society handle that you just eliminated age barriers!

There are so many amazing women and men kicking butt and taking names! There are so many that are living their best lives and not apologizing for their age or, quite possibly, for the fact that they didn't get an early start! There are no two people that are the same! People have different timelines and circumstances when it comes to accomplishing their dreams!

Breakthrough the program and unleash your unlimited potential! Do the things that you thought you had to hang up because some call you "over-the-hill!" Who cares what those dream killers have to say anyway! Go out and prove them wrong! Show them that you are unshakeable and not be stopped! Just like a bouy, bounce back and keep on keeping on! I believe in you!

Write Your Goals Down!

"Sit down and write it down with a pen and then make up your mind you are going to do it. Don't spend any time thinking of why you can't. The fun is not in getting it, the fun is in growing. Goals are to help us grow, goals are to help us get. The getting is a site benefit; the growth is the real benefit."
-Bob Proctor

It has been proven that you are more likely to achieve your goals if you write them down! Committing your vision to paper takes a dream and makes it. From there, you can work on dividing your dream up into baby steps to accomplish your goal. If you don't break your vision into baby steps, your goal can seem overwhelming and daunting, and like you don't know where to start. But if you break it down into baby steps, you will begin to see yourself making progress before you know it!

For years, I told myself that I would write a book, but I never even put my thoughts to paper. I told myself that I didn't have a topic to write about and that I didn't have time! That's a crock of crap! I did have the time, and I did have something to write about. The subject matter that makes up this book is something I am VERY PASSIONATE about! I have seen many people struggle and live lives of anger and negativity. I just knew deep in my soul that wasn't the life for me.

When I finally forced myself to sit down and conquer a couple of pages at a time. It not only seemed like something I could do but something I could do for the rest of my life. Every day, I would write how many pages I would write in my intentions and reflections journal that day. I found immense joy in accomplishing my daily intention because it was something that I alone had control of, and I did not have to rely on others for me to write my pages!

Write down your goals. Remind yourself of where you are headed multiple times a day. Don't let anything throw you off. If you have to readjust your goals or manipulate them, so they fit your thoughts, your personal growth, and your current life situation, by all means, do so. Your goals may change, and that's alright. Not everything is going to work out exactly as you planned. The road to success is not a linear path! It's filled with ups and downs, dead ends, speed bumps, and dead carcasses laying in the street. The odds are that your dreams will have to be modified at some point. Continue to write them down and read them multiple times a day, regardless.

It's said that the best time to do this is when you wake and right before bed. I say, do that if you can and if it works for you, but if it doesn't, work it into your schedule somewhere else in your day.

People who write their goals down are more likely to achieve them and even more likely to achieve them if they have someone they know holding them accountable. When it comes to this, I would caution you to be careful who you select as your accountability partner! You do not want to share your goals and dreams with a dementor or dream killer! Make sure this is someone who will cheer you on without being jealous. Make sure this is someone that you know, like, and trust.

Oprah has always said that Gayle has been such a fantastic friend to her for many reasons, but one of those reasons is that she was never envious of Oprah (except I guess when she got to perform with Tina Turner.) Know that's a true friend, and that's someone that you can have as an accountability partner. You want someone cheering you on and someone who isn't worried about you outshining them because they are perfectly comfortable living in their light.

I will happily admit that I have a good group of girlfriends who do the same for me. At times, I think they believe in me and see more potential in myself than I do. I love that about them. When I think of quitting, settling, or being subpar, I fear that I may let them down. My rational mind comes in to tell me that I could never let them down. They just want me to be happy, healthy, and well.

These are the people you need to surround yourself with and have as accountability partners. You want people who will give it to you straight, and you want to make sure you have someone who won't sugarcoat things or lie to you. When you don't accomplish what you set out to, you want someone to tell you. When you are blinded and can't see what's going on in your life, you also want someone to tell you that.

Write your goals down and share them with quality people that you know, like, and trust!

Don't Let Anyone Tell You That You Can't Do Something! Where You Start is Not Where You are Going to End Up!

"Millionaires when they are told they can't do something find a way up, around, through, or under."
-Michael Sandler from Inspire Nation Podcast

As a child, Dr. John Frederick Demartini couldn't read, and he wrote backwards. He even had to wear a dunce cap in class. His teacher called his parents and basically told them that he can't read, he writes backwards, and that he will never be anything, do anything or go anywhere with his life. And that maybe they should think about getting him involved in sports because she could tell that he enjoyed running. Well, boy, was she wrong! Now, he has a net worth of 10 million and is the author of 40 books (at the time of this writing) published in 29 different languages.

"What lies behind us and what lies before us are small matters compared to what lies within us." – Ralph Waldo Emerson

John Frederick Demartini believes the first step in your journey to becoming financially independent is ridding yourself of shame, guilt, and the feeling that you are undeserving. That is the first and most significant thing that is holding you back in your journey to manifest the life of your dreams! You don't want to get caught up in beating yourself up and letting negative thoughts about yourself consume you.

The second thing he advises is to find a way to serve. So many people walk around wondering what's in it for them. When the mindset of the wealthy is more along the lines of how-may-I-serve-thee? He says that you need to value wealth and service and value not spending every dime you get. Your values must be more aligned with saving and investing your money. If your values are in spending the money you earn, it will leave you just as fast as it comes. Demartini states that money circulates in the economy from those who value it least to those who value it most. It makes sense, right?

Having an automatic savings intact is a step in the right direction. Plus, your values need to be in alignment with your end goal. You need to be dedicated and disciplined. Your thoughts, words, and actions all need to line up with each other, which is not easy. The world has many temptations that distract us from reaching the highest, truest expression of ourselves. Perhaps, that is why so few people achieve financial independence.

Every human being lives by a set of priorities and values, Demartini points out. When people set goals that are in alignment with their highest goals and values, he says, "they become the most powerful and effective people they can be." Now, isn't that how you would like people to describe you? The most powerful and effective (insert name here) you that you can be? I would like to be described as such. When they are in this state of being, he states that people are the most grateful, most disciplined, most resilient, and fulfilled. When we are young, the disciplined life doesn't seem so appealing, and as we grow older, we see the most successful people leading lives of discipline, and it doesn't seem all that bad. Well, good news, it's not so bad. Really! Self-discipline over time leads to self-confidence and happiness, I have found!

Negative things such as procrastination, frustration, hesitation, and being a victim of your past, he finds will keep you poor and not living up to the highest most authentic expression of you. Those things will also keep you from reaching financial independence. You are in the driver's seat of your own life! Take the wheel!

Look at what the people you are surrounding yourself with are focusing their time on. Look at their discipline. Look at their passions. And look at whether they are organized or not. Look at where they spend their money and where their energy comes from. Watch their words and what inspires them, and what their goals are. Look at what they take an interest in learning more about.

Primarily, the goal is to find a mission or life's work that will make you spring out of bed every morning with enthusiasm to start your day and tackle the tasks at hand. And as you probably already know...it's not the same for everybody. Some people find this out very quickly and early in their lives, and for some, it takes longer. However long it takes you, work on finding this. It is amazing.

Find something that is of value to you but also is of value to other people. There you will find success and happiness.

The ancient Greeks called living by your highest value or the highest priority in life "Telos." That is what you are meant to do in this life. John Frederick Demartini says that you are most resilient and adaptable to pain and pleasure when you do. Fill your life with things that are meaningful to you.

Make sure your goals are attainable and set reasonable goals and action steps to help you achieve them. Everyday, visualize and keep your focus on what you intend to do and who you intend to become. Start with simple goals and find victory in those. If you can get into the habit of doing what you say you will do, Demartini says, your wealth will begin to grow.So, start with small goals and small achievable action steps and keep building from there. Take the big goal and slice it up into little achievable bits in which you can measure your progress. Then, stick with your goal long enough, and sooner or later, you will have the success you have been longing for!

Following that, John Frederick says that you have to prove that you can micromanage before macro-manage. What he is saying is that you need to take steps towards your goal a little each day. As most of you and I know, there is no such thing as an overnight success. Most people that are considered an overnight success have been working at their craft for about 15 years or so! So, just focus on taking baby steps!

"The sculpture is already complete within the marble block before I start my work. It is already there, I just have to chisel away the superfluous material." — Michelangelo

You and your goals and dreams are that sculpture. And you taking baby steps towards your goal day in and day out is like Michaelangelo chipping away relentlessly at the block of marble.

You and your highest truest version of yourself is just waiting to be released from the stone and put on display for the world to gaze at in amazement!

"Inch by inch, life's a cinch. Yard by yard, life's hard." — John Bytheway

Breaking your goal down into doable steps is so important. Doing this helps, so it doesn't seem as if the task is looming over you. When I started to write my book, I told myself that I would just write for one hour that day. The next day I said to myself that I would write for 3 hours, and then I thought to myself...'What if my goal is to write ten pages a day?' That would be 70 pages a week. 140 pages in 2 weeks and 210 pages in three weeks. Then I got excited, and it became a sort of game to me! I thought, 'Three weeks and I can almost have a rough draft of an entire book? Sign me up!' Perhaps, that is a great way to think of things, make it fun! Make it a game! Make it a competition with yourself and never compare yourself to others! They are not running the same race as you!

Did you know that 70% of Americans say they don't like their jobs? It's a shame that so many people are living lives of quiet desperation.

Suze Orman as a child, had a speech impediment and was not a good reader. When meeting with her college advisor, she said that she wanted to be a brain surgeon, and they told her she didn't have the grades for that. She was supposed to graduate from college but hadn't fulfilled her language requirement due to her shame of being poor at English. She left there. She borrowed some money from her brother and set out to see America with some of her girlfriends.

Eventually, she became a waitress at the buttercup bakery. And finally went back to school to finish her degree. After several years passed, she decided to own her own restaurant but didn't have the money. One of her regulars that she had been waiting on for 6 years, heard her story of wanting to own her own restaurant and piled some money together with the other customers and gave her a bunch of checks which collectively added up to $50,000.00 to be paid back in 10 years, if she could, zero interest. Fred, her regular, told her to take the money down and invest it at Merrill Lynch. Because of what her investor Randy had done, she lost all her money in three months.

She was interviewed to be a broker. The man who interviewed her told her that women should be barefoot and pregnant while working there, so she sued Merrill Lynch. Eventually, she paid the money back to those people who lent it to her.

But that's another thing, do not give up on your way to success. Suze Orman wanted to own a restaurant and made $400.00 a month as a waitress at the buttercup bakery. She probably never dreamed of the great career in financial advising that she has now. With a net worth of between 10 and 30 million. She is a financial advisor, author, and a podcast host. That just goes to show you that you can do anything you set your mind to! It's not the circumstances that you are born into and it's up to you to write your own story and do things your way! Make the life you want! Blaze your own trail! You might just surprise yourself and become someone beyond your wildest dreams!

While writing this book, I realized that I had fallen victim to this, too! I had always wanted to model. Like many others I believed that you had to be tall and skinny to model. I thought that I was too short and too curvy. I also thought that if I admitted to others, I wanted to model that I might come across as vain and self-centered for wanting other people to take my pictures and look at my pictures and order merchandise with them.

One day in early June 2019, I was at the beach with my friends, and I had this red bikini top on, red lipstick, and jet-black hair. I asked my friend, Caroline, if she wouldn't mind taking several pictures of me. One of them turned out so well that I ended up posting it to my personal Instagram with the caption, SI 2020. SI meaning Sports Illustrated.

I went to see my friend, Ashley, at her home sometime within that same week. I showed her the photos and made jokes about the caption I posted. And she said something along the lines of why *are you making jokes? You could model. Kim Kardashian is about the same height as you. She's not tall. And she's curvy. What makes you think that you can't do it, too.* Well, that was all it took. That was the year I gave up on telling myself and the world why I wasn't good enough and started modeling. That year, I sold my first calendar with pictures from my modeling, and I sold black and white posters of one of my favorite shots.

Who knows how much money I will generate in the long run from my modeling or where it will take me? Or if it's going to be a long-term career of mine. All I know is I'm glad I tried it and stopped accepting the limitations and constraints that others put on it! Go me!

Birds of a Feather

"You are the average of the five people you spend the most time with." -Jim Rohn

Have you ever heard the saying, "birds of a feather flock together?" Well, it's a saying for a reason, and they say you become most like the five people you spend the most time with. And they say that you make within $5,000.00 of the people you spend the most time with. So, look at your inner circle. Are you hanging around with deadbeats and people you know aren't good for you? Well, today is the day you stop spending time with them and go and get yourself a new set of friends.

I know you're like, *but Anna these people have been there for me.* Well, continue staying around them if you want to live the rest of your life where you're at. If you want more, you have to become more. If your friends and loved ones aren't pushing you or encouraging you to be all that you can be, they aren't for you! Seriously, it's time to hang around people that have good habits and people who are further along than you. Let them teach you and learn from them. Observe them and ask questions. Most people are more than willing to help. Most people like people who like them, too.

You want to surround yourself with people on the same mission as you. Happy people, caring people, motivated people. People who are going to be there to be honest with you and help you become the highest version of yourself. If someone tells you that you can't do something or laughs at your dreams, they are not someone that you should be around. If they are in trouble, in and out of jail, and are still making the same decisions (after the first time, it's no longer a mistake), they aren't for you. If someone you are friends with doesn't respect your belongings or can't follow through on what they promised, they also aren't for you.

I can't speak for you, men. But for us women, I would say listen to your gut. Listen to that little voice inside of you that knows when something isn't right. When you are around someone, and they make you feel miserable, odds are that person is not aiding you in becoming your highest self. If you don't trust someone but have no evidence, trust your gut. Now, I am not promoting being mean to someone or attacking them personally, but you need to know when one chapter of the book ends and another begins. And you need to know who was meant to be in your life for a reason, a season, and/or a lifetime.

It's important to associate yourself with people who want to see you succeed and not people who will drag you down. Very important.

Dr. Bruce Lipton recalls when he became a developmental cellar biologist. In his graduate work, he cloned stem cells. He points out that everyone believes stem cells to be a rather new discovery in science when really, he was working with stem cells in 1967, so they aren't as new as what everyone believes them to be. But the real story here is what he learned from working with these cells and how it relates to our surroundings and our environment.

Dr. Lipton would put cells into the priti dish and they would divide and multiply. After about two weeks, he had thousands of cells in the petri dish but what he claimed to be unique is, "they were all genetically identical." Because of his findings he transferred some of the cells that he had grown and put them in a dish with a COMPLETELY DIFFERENT ENVIRONMENT. And the results were astounding. Do you know what happened? The stem cells adapted to their environment, which was a dish full of muscle cells. The same result occurred when the stem cells were transplanted into a container with bone, and a third dish, fat cells, became those cells. If you move cells from a healthy environment into a bad environment, the cells get sick. And when the cells get sick, the cool thing about it is that they don't need any medicine at all; what they need is to be put back into a healthy environment. Then they become well again.

It is easy to conclude from his experiment that we are all products of our environment, and we must be very mindful and cautious of who and what we surround ourselves with. If you run with losers, you will most certainly end up a loser. If you hang with kids at the top of your class, odds are your grades will improve. If you hang out with the heavy hitters and the leaders of your career field, odds are some of that will rub off on you. So, be careful when it comes to who and what you have around you. It could make or break you. There is no doubt.

As he was doing this research and discovering this information, Dr. Lipton was teaching conventional material out of the textbook, i.e. genes control the science. And it was then he found himself faced with quite the dilemma. It was going against all his moral values teaching this information when he had recently discovered it to be untrue. He decided he could not keep his integrity and teach something that he found to be wrong. Even though he had tenure at the University, he walked out.

Dr. Bruce says that when you teach that the genes control life, you teach victimization and that you can't control what happens to you and because of his research and his experiences he knows that's not true. He has been teaching people for decades that you can control your life. The genes are not, and it's up to you to manifest changes and change your perceptions so you can create what you desire.

Cells adapted to the environment they were in. This proves to people, perhaps you don't need to be taking as many prescription drugs. Perhaps, you or your loved one isn't as bad as you originally thought. Change the environment, and people change, cells change. Dr. Bruce Lipton has also proved that you are not a victim of your genes. You have power over your genes. He's been going around teaching people about epigenetics. Epi meaning above. Epigenetics meaning above the genes. So, stop being a victim. Change your physical environment. Get in a better neighborhood, perhaps. Change the people you associate yourself with if you find that they are holding you back. Remember that you and you alone are in charge of your life. Stop pointing fingers and placing blame. Now is the time to start taking some responsibility.

Don't Focus on Your Fears, Focus on Your Desires

"Faith and fear both demand that you believe in something you cannot see. You choose!"
-Bob Proctor

Your fears will consume you and immobilize you. Most people make lame excuses about why they haven't started.

Ever notice that when you focus on the negative things that are wrong with someone or something, it becomes this toxic and unhealthy spiral? And when you start focusing on all the good in your life, your day continues to get better and better and better? Well, that's not a coincidence.

This part of the book touches partially on something that I touched on earlier in the book, where I discuss using your spirituality to help you overcome the great storms of life. I don't think people realize the effect that fear has on their lives. I believe that fear is almost as strong or a stronger emotion than love. Fear can allow us to be manipulated and do things we wouldn't normally do. It can also paralyze us and keep us from doing anything at all.

Fear vs. Desires reminds me of the old Cherrokee story, *The Story of Two Wolves*. It goes like this:

An old Cherokee is teaching his grandson about life. "A fight is going on inside me," he said to the boy. "It is a terrible fight, and it is between two wolves. One is evil – he is anger, envy, sorrow, regret, greed, arrogance, self-pity, guilt, resentment, inferiority, lies, false pride, superiority, and ego."

He continued, "The other is good – he is joy, peace, love, hope, serenity, humility, kindness, benevolence, empathy, generosity, truth, compassion, and faith. The same fight is going on inside you – and inside every other person, too."

The grandson thought about it for a minute and then asked his grandfather, "Which wolf will win?"

The old Cherokee simply replied, "The one you feed."

We ultimately choose whether we want to focus on our fears or focus on our desires. The fear, if you focus on it, will consume you and dictate your behavior. Your desires will do pretty much the same. However, the emotions, thoughts, and chemical reactions within the body are completely different.

Start focusing on your goals, dreams, and desires, and stop focusing on what could go wrong. People may laugh at you; they may call you names. But usually, those people are not actively putting themselves out there, requiring of themselves that they be vulnerable. As Brene Brown teaches, it takes great courage and strength to be vulnerable and put yourself out there. So, if you are or if you do, kudos to you for being so brave!

Focus on your desires and ride the excitement of them like a way. Make sure you're practicing your affirmations, incantations, and visualizations daily. Pump yourself up and psych yourself into being all you were created to be! You have a purpose! And you can help others and be of service when you put your gifts and talents to use!

Be Careful How You Define Yourself!

"When you judge another, you do not define them, you define yourself." -Dr. Wayne Dyer

There was a time in my life where I was out of shape, and I was not satisfied that the clothes that I loved no longer fit and so on. One day I was cleaning the drawers in my kitchen, and I found a vinyl decal that my mom had given me: an oval with the number 13.1 to symbolize the accomplishment of running a half marathon, which I had done a couple of times. I had a similar decal on my white Ford Explorer that I used to drive, but I now owned a red Ford Fusion, I no longer had a sticker that displayed my accomplishment. I knew I needed to get back running and get back in shape. I had transformed my physical body multiple times through running. Running gives me increased energy and a greater sense of self-confidence. So, I decided to put the decal back on my car because I knew that I would be defining myself as an athlete if I did.

When I stepped out of my vehicle, I wanted my physical form to match the vinyl decal on my bumper. I didn't want people to scratch their heads and witness a dichotomy. I wanted them to see that

I am an athlete and I love to run. That I could have power over my mind when my body told me it wanted to quit. And wouldn't you know, after I put the decal on my car, I started running more often and getting back into shape.

That is just one example of the correlation between our behaviors and who we define ourselves as. If you tell yourself you are a doctor, odds are you will complete the eight years of schooling needed, overcome the obstacles and have a successful medical career. If you tell yourself you are a felon, and you will always be a felon, odds are you will continue the behavior that a felon would. If you are a cheater and you call yourself one you will always act the part. If you define yourself as a millionaire, you will not participate in activities that millionaires don't participate in. You become your definition.

Knowing this, I encourage you to define yourself in a way that you must grow, evolve, and strive in order to fit the requirements of your definition. If you define yourself as a kind person, you won't find yourself lashing out in anger. If you describe yourself as hospitable, you will always have people filling your home with love and laughter. If you define yourself as generous, perhaps you will become a philanthropist. Please, be very careful how you define yourself because your behavior will support your definition.

Proverbs 18:21: Death and life are in the power of the tongue, And those who love it will eat its fruit. -New American Standard Bible

As humans, we have known for quite some time now about the power of our words. We know what impact they have on our lives. But, we still fall victim to using negative words to describe ourselves and then acting out that description. They say *when you know better you do better*. And it is time for us to start doing better. It is so crucial for us to do so.

Since the internet was created, we have a vast amount of knowledge literally at our fingertips. If we have a question within seconds, we have an answer. If we wonder if anyone has had a similar experience, we can probably find someone who has been through the same thing. So, it is time to stop defining ourselves as something we don't want to be.

It is time to declare that we are in favor. That we are overwhelmed with blessings. That we are experiencing overwhelming abundance and all our dreams are coming true. We are accomplishing great things.

Train your thoughts and your speech to serve you. Not to hinder your progress and hold you back! It's a must!

Plan Everything

"Failing to plan is planning to fail." – Alan Lakein

Even if you plan to have a completely spontaneous and unplanned night with your significant other, make sure you have a time block for that in your calendar. LeAnn Rimes once recorded a song called *Nothin' Better to Do*. In the song, one of the lyrical lines went as follows, 'Mama said, "Idle hands are Devil's handiwork".' Over the years, I have found very little to be more accurate. Whenever I find myself having nothing to do or lacking purpose, trouble always seems to find me. As it does with others, I can attest to that.

Another benefit of planning is that you manage your time better. When you sit down on Sunday and take time to plan out your whole week, you will be amazed at how much time that you are currently wasting. Even if you think you are a productive person, I GUARANTEE that you are not utilizing the time you have at hand to its full potential.

We get sucked into things like social media and television. Do you know how much time we spend making other people rich? That monthly subscription to Netflix could buy you online classes, to help you get closer to achieving your goals and dreams, and instead, you are making some actor, producer and director more money. And don't get me wrong, supporting our artists or entertaining yourself is okay but in MODERATION. Some people spend way too much time on social media. I must check myself when it comes to this. You don't realize how much time you are spending in a day just every once and a while checking into Facebook or Instagram for a couple of mins, scrolling through your feed, liking pictures, and commenting on engagement posts. You are why people get so much business from Facebook ads and why there is such a thing as Instagram Influencers. These are on good days. Some days, if you don't truly love yourself, you can become a victim of self-deprecating thoughts and constantly compare yourself to someone else's state of bliss that they "appear" to be in. Remember that people don't always post all the hard stuff.

    Planning will also save you from boredom. You won't have time to be bored. Each waking hour of your day will be designed with duties and tasks.

    Make your schedule your friend. Plan the life you have always dreamed of. And if you can't do that, break your dreams down into little baby steps and do a little each day. It makes a big goal less overwhelming, and before you know it you will be closer to your goal than you think.

Procrastination Kills

"'Cause sometimes someday just never comes."
-Someday, a song by Alan Jackson

Procrastination is a result of an unclear vision or, sometimes, a feeling of overwhelm. If you don't break your vision down into achievable, doable, measurable goals, then you are going to feel as if you are standing at the bottom of a mountain with no hiking boots. Have a clear vision. Use your calendar to your advantage. Make time, my friend. Start each day with purpose and intention.

Brian Tracy is author of a book called, *Eat That Frog*. This book addresses the main thing that makes us fall prey to procrastination. Most of the time, us individuals have several important things to do in a day and more than likely, one out of those several tasks is something that we don't particularly want to do. I believe this is what makes most people procrastinators. Perhaps, you must fire someone at work, give your boss your two-weeks notice, sit down and do your chemistry homework. Whatever it is that we seem to be not particularly fond of, we put off. And you cannot do this if you wish to be successful. Take the hardest task or the task you like the least and move it to the top of your to-do list. Do it first and get it out of the way. It will keep it from looming over you the entire day and stressing you out just by thinking about it.

A lot of us could have a better quality of life if we just overcame procrastination. And I will admit, I am not perfect, and I can fall prey to procrastination at times, too but we have to work on this constantly. Hold yourself accountable. How many areas of our life would we improve simply by eliminating procrastination? Odds are you would have a better body, a better marriage. You could learn that language or write that book! We have so many excuses on why now isn't a good time. Well, sometimes it will be more ideal than others but if you are always looking for a way out of doing something, one excuse or another will always be there.

At times, I will even find myself trying to procrastinate when it comes to doing something I love! How bizarre is that? And I know you know what I am talking about. For example, I would procrastinate writing this book even though I bleed this positive-thinking-motivation-you-can-do-it-shit! Regardless of that being so, I still had to make myself sit down and write every morning. And make a goal for how many pages I would complete that day. But you want to know something cool? Once I started writing, I loved it! And I didn't want to stop! But every day, I had to talk myself into getting started.

Long-story-short is, procrastination can be very deceiving. I think it's our mind trying to keep us safe and engaged in our "normal." That way nothing is a threat. But if we stay the same, there are no opportunities to grow. So, procrastination can be very dangerous, and I will admit that once you complete a task, you can get so addicted to that feeling of accomplishment and since of pride! It just feels so good!

Have Some Kind of Belief System

"There is no right or wrong path. There is only the path you choose. Whatever you choose, there will be many opportunities for you to grow and expand." -Kuan Yin

When it comes to the spiritual/religious realm…there is no right or wrong way to go about it. As long as you are not in a cult or hurting anyone and you believe that what you believe in is helping you become a wiser, kinder, and more generous person. Rock on, my friend!

I was raised Catholic and remember as a child sitting on the carpet of Our Lady of the Lakes, flipping through the old, fat, green hymnal. Before I could even read the words on the page or the notes, I knew I wanted to sing. I was in choir in college and would sing in the churches and cathedrals in Grand Rapids, Mi. I had some resistance growing up to the Catholic Church because some of their beliefs were not my own. I wanted my mother to understand that even if I didn't identify as a Catholic, I still had a belief system that would help shape me and mold me into the woman I am today and the woman I will be tomorrow.

I studied world religion in high school, which opened my eyes to a world that I was never exposed to in my earlier years. I learned about Hinduism and Buddhism and how Buddha wasn't fat, and how after his message traveled up the silk trade routes to China, you had one plump man. I credit it to something very similar to the game of telephone.

It was then that I started to see that all the religions were teaching the same things: respect your elders, give generously, be kind, listen, forgive, have empathy, honor your parents, be thankful, everything happens for a reason, life is cyclical, etc. They just go about teaching you this in different ways. And their storylines pick up and drop off at different points in history. The details are different, but the message is pretty much the same. LOVE YOUR NEIGHBOR BECAUSE WE AREN'T THAT DIFFERENT.

Life will knock you down. Les Brown says, "When life knocks you down, try to land on your back. Because if you can look up, you can get up." It will hit you hard when you least expect it to. It will hit you when you are flying high, and feeling mean. It will knock down what you have been building. Life will make you question what you once professed to know.

In the process of writing this book, I suffered a great loss. It made me question what I thought I knew, my future, and my past. The loss took a great toll on me emotionally. But it forced me to realign and refocus. The loss I suffered made it even more important to me that I reached my goals and started living and working towards the life I always dreamed of. I started waking up early and reading my bible, praying and meditating. I started taking better care of my body through diet and exercise. I stopped over indulging in pleasures and forced myself to become more self-disciplined.

Don't ever think that you are unable to withstand the storm that you are currently experiencing. God (or whatever name you use for our creator or the divine) will not give you anything you cannot handle. That is being used to mold you and shape you and prepare you for what is to come. Instead of saying, *why is this happening to me?* Ask, *what can I learn from this?* Let this time of hardship that you are going through become your teacher. Let yourself emerge from the storm stronger because of it.

Even though I never played video games, pretend your life is like a game, and once you overcome the challenges of the first level, you earn more points and graduate to the second level. Odds are if you can't survive the first level, you won't be able to kick ass when you get to the more advanced level. Keep that in mind, when it comes to life. Don't become discouraged by the problem. Know that the pain is only temporary. Eric Thomas, ET,

The Hip-Hop Preacher, has a quote that I love, and it goes, "Pain is temporary. It may last for a minute, or an hour or a day, or even a year. But eventually, it will subside. And something else will take its place. If I quit, however, it will last forever."

That is so true! Pain doesn't last forever. Look to your spiritual guides for guidance on what you should do moving forward. Practice good morals and ethics to help you get where you are going. And as for the people that hurt you, do your best to be kind to them. Odds are they are hurting too! Your pain will subside. Your days will get better! Keep on believing! Keep on showing up! Don't let them count you out so easily! You can do this! You are one tough cookie!

Often when hardships hit, I just try to slow everything down and only approach life at small time increments that I can handle. Sometimes, it's day by day. Other times, it's week by week or month by month. That doesn't matter. Just have your eyes focused on the prize (your dream) and do/be the best you can.

We are all human. We stumble. We fail. We fall. We make mistakes. But we mustn't quit. Deep down in your heart, you know that you are special and have gifts and talents that no one else possesses quite the way you do! It's okay if you are experiencing hardships and challenges, I don't know if I believe anymore that life is supposed to be easy. What I do know is, it's worth it. And we can't quit on our dreams. We must persevere through the troubling times and come out the other side improved. Let it transform you!

On the journey to becoming our highest, truest self, we will face obstacles. We must not cower and bow down to them. Instead, we need to put our fears aside and face them head on!

When I used to live in Michigan with my parents, I could often find my mom binge-watching John Wayne movies on a Saturday morning, dreaming of being "The Duke's" lady and what it would be like to live in the wild west. My mom loved John Wayne. My aunt one year gifted her a mug with a picture of him on it and a quote that read, "Courage is being scared to death, but saddling up anyway." I always loved that quote. I know during times of hardship, we can be afraid of the unknown and scared of the foreseeable future and what it may hold. But what courage is, is carrying on despite the fear that's tempting you from moving forward. That fear can be immobilizing, and we cannot let it immobilize us or keep us from reaching our goals, hopes, and dreams!

You are a creator, just like your creator! Start believing in your divine powers and your ability to make a positive impact and focus your sights on doing good! Don't let yourself sulk. Take the time you need to grieve, and then get back on that horse! You have to be looking for a solution and healing! Let your spiritual/religious beliefs help aid you in this endeavor!

Play Tennis with a Better Player

"Don't surround yourself with people who just affirm you. Surround yourself with people who challenge you." -Tony Robbins

Like the late great comedic television actress Carol Burnett said, "Always play tennis with a better player because your game only improves every time." And while this is true for tennis, it applies to all aspects and areas of your life. If you need help organizing and you have a friend that loves to clean and is extremely organized, invite them over to help you and show you a thing or two. If you want to make more money, start hanging out with people who make more money. Start going to the wealthy part of town and window shopping there until you can afford to buy what they sell in those kinds of stores and while you're window shopping don't focus on your lack. Focus on the abundance that surrounds you.

If you would like to switch careers and get paid to work in a specialty, that is your passion. Start hanging out with people who make a living doing what you want to do. I was working as an administrative assistant in Nashville, and a server at an Italian restaurant, and I wanted music to be my life. So, I started hanging out and spending more time with people who didn't have a 9 to 5 and people who played, taught, and performed music all the time.

Your environment rubs off on you. They say that you are the sum of the five people you spend the most time with. Don't want to be broke? Don't hang out with broke people. Spend your time with people who are doing better than you in one way or another.

Decide What It Is You Want & Accept Nothing Less

*"The minute you settle for less than you deserve,
You get even less than you settled for."*
-Maureen Dowd

If you want your music to have a certain sound, don't listen to Joe Schmo! It's your music! Listen to your heart and soul and do what you think is right. I'm a singer, and I write songs, as well. My songs aren't as mainstream as others are and I have been told, plenty of times, that if I want my music to get on the radio, I have to change my style and write differently than I do. As an artist, I have decided that I am not going to compromise who I am or what I believe in for the sake of getting my music on the radio. Does that mean that I can't learn to write in a style that's popular? Of course not. It is always fun to learn about new things. Especially for me, when it comes to music, I believe that today's mainstream writers are very talented. It takes a lot to create a unique work of art within a specific formula. But I have decided for my music that I will write my songs as I would like them to be, and if one happens to get picked up by a famous artist, it does, and if not, that is fine.

So many times, people settle for less than they originally set out for, hoped for or planned for. I see it happening a lot in romantic relationships and jobs. Someone told you that you couldn't be a lawyer because your IQ or grades weren't high enough so, you believed them and quit before you even tried. Who are they to tell you? I see it with romantic relationships. People know what they want and how they deserve to be treated but they are so afraid of being alone. Sometimes it isn't even the fear of being alone, and sometimes it's simply the fear of the unknown that trips people up. Know what you want and accept nothing less. **"Raise your standards,"** as Tony Robbins would say.

Get Quiet

"My imagination functions much better when I don't have to speak to people."
— Patricia Highsmith

Ever noticed that all your good ideas come to you when you are in the shower or driving? I know why that is. Your mind gets quiet enough, and the task you are performing is being taken care of by your subconscious mind, basically on autopilot. You can't be doing too many other things when you are in the shower or driving. So, your mind lets in thoughts and ideas that it can't let in when you have too much mental clutter going on.

I get great ideas for songs when I am driving or in the shower or I'm getting ready for bed, winding down.

That is why prayer and meditation are so important. It allows us to quiet our minds in such a busy and chaotic world. I will admit I am still working on mastering both. And I need to implement these into my daily routine. But when I do them, I notice a difference.

Let Go of Control

"Trying to control leads to ruin" -Dr. Wayne Dyer, Change Your Thoughts, Change Your Life

Ever noticed when you're at the beach that if you pick up sand and leave your hand open, the sand stays in your palm? But if you close your fingers and make a fist, the sand slips through your fingers. That is exactly like life. Life should flow and be easy. If you're feeling intense resistance or restraint, odds are you need to take a step back, look at your life and change what it is that you believe needs to be changed. Trying to make someone stay in your life is also the same as closing your fist with sand. I know. I have experienced this firsthand (haha – no pun intended).

Learn to welcome the things that are meant for you and let go of those that aren't.

Body Language

"Effective communication is 20% what you know and 80% how you feel about what you know."
-Jim Rohn

Believe it or not we could probably write a whole book about you solely based on your body language. Are your shoulders rounded and sagged, or do you thrust your shoulders back and sit up? When someone is speaking to you do you listen intently to what they are saying by maintaining eye contact, furrowing your brows if you are confused, smiling or laughing when they say something funny, leaning in and listening with intent and asking questions according to the conversation?

When you speak, are people straining to hear your words, or do you speak loud enough for others to hear you and what you have to say? Or do you start to speak your mind, or present an idea to your family members or co-workers but before you can finish iterating the idea do you wave your hand and dismiss what you were saying as "stupid," all the while shaking your head? These things affect others' perception of you and their perception of what you believe to be true about yourself.

People can quickly tell when you are interested, uninterested, confident or insecure. What are you projecting? What are people's first impressions of you? It might be beneficial to ask people (who you think will be honest and open and kind) their first impression of you. If you start to see a trend maybe there is something to examine and work on.

You can also do this through intense mirror work, which the late and great Louise Hay was so fond of. If you are high in self-awareness, I would recommend this. Perhaps, you can try both. Do you normally smile or grimace? Do you seem approachable to others? That is very important. A lot of life is building and maintaining relationships and about who you know and attract to you. Body language plays a more significant role than what you know.

Say "When" Not "If"

Certainty: a fact that is definitely true or an event that is definitely going to take place.

If is one of those horrible words you need to eliminate from your vocabulary, especially when you are talking about yourself. Now, don't go back through this book and highlight and count the number of times I use the word "if" throughout these pages. That's not what I'm after. I am after taking the word "if" out of your vocabulary when talking about what you would like to manifest in your life.

I don't want to hear you say, "If I make the basketball team…" I want to hear you say, "WHEN I make the basketball team…" You need to believe in yourself! You need to declare your future! Throughout this whole book I have been talking to you about the power of your beliefs, thoughts, energy and actions. But something I need to drive home before this book is over is the power of your words, the power of speech.

"Develop your communication skills because when you open your mouth, you tell the world who you are." -Les Brown

Do you want the world to know you are average or do you want to tell the world you are a champion and you intend to conquer! Do you want to tell the world that you are confident and that you believe in yourself or that you don't know how to love yourself and consider yourself undeserving?

You want to say, "When I get that promotion," "When I marry the love of my life," "When I touch thousands with my charitable endeavors!" Using the word "If" makes what you are saying sound weak and like you don't believe that you and the divine can work in harmony to manifest and attain such a thing. And if you don't believe or think you deserve what you want, why should anyone else? Convince yourself. Convince others with how you speak and act.

There are other words that you should eliminate from your vocabulary, if you haven't yet. For instance, "Wish," "But," "Should." There is this amazing quote that I came across one time having to do with the word, "should." It goes something like this, *and should makes prisoner of us all.* To this day, I am not sure who said it and if anyone knows please feel free to contact me. What I like about it is the intense imagery that shows what we do to ourselves mentally and emotionally every time we use the word, "Should." I would highly advise just getting rid of it altogether. You will be happier when you do.

My Grammy

"I had a boyfriend who told me I'd never succeed, never be nominated for a Grammy, never have a hit song, and that he hoped I'd fail. I said to him, 'Someday, when we're not together, you won't be able to order a cup of coffee at the fucking deli without hearing or seeing me." -Lady Gaga

Well, you may not believe this, as I write this, I can honestly say that I do not have a Grammy…yet. And I mean exactly what I said, "I don't have my Grammy…yet!" No, I'm not nominated, and nor has a famous artist recorded my song…yet. But what I will tell you is something my dad always said, "Walk through life with a good heart and you will run with success."

I will keep holding fast to my dreams and working hard on my craft, and cherishing my relationships, and I will get there. You will be sitting on the couch one day shoving popcorn in your mouth, in your pajamas. You will see me accept my award and you will be like, *well, I'll be damned. She did it!* :)

Afterthoughts

"Your circumstances have very little to do with your fulfillment in life. It's how you're approaching your circumstances, your attitude toward your circumstances that make a difference in the world."
-Dr. Wayne Dyer

One thing I learned about myself when writing this book is that I am a terrible speller! Haha, but it's okay, I'm getting better day in and day out. I just want to say what a pleasure it was writing this book. I would like to thank you from the bottom of my heart for taking time out of your busy schedules to read it. I hope this book inspires you and motivates you to live and become the highest, truest version of yourself. I hope that you exceed your expectations. I hope your life is a joy and a pleasure. I have realized that each day is a gift and even better when we're present. Take time to play and be stupid with your dog. Don't forget to say I love you and express your gratitude.

My life turned out differently than I expected it to be as a child, but I love it. I love the process of evolution and cannot wait to see where this journey takes me. I hope this book brings happiness and joy to your life. And I hope you learned something. I wish you all the best. And I can't say it enough, thank you!

"As a man thinks in his heart, so is he." -Dr. Wayne Dyer

"The most difficult project in the world is the reconstruction of the human mind."

"You are the sum total of all you have been **conditioned** to think."

"What we see and what we hear are small things compared to what we think."

"The thinking of the mind changes only when we conceive what we believe and accept what we hear."

"The most powerful force on earth is the will of man."

"The goal of oppression is a broken spirit."

Sources for "Be Delusional"
A Book Written by: Anna Rose Egres

http://www.todayifoundout.com/index.php/2014/04/colonel-sanders-actually-colonel/
https://www.businessinsider.com/what-successful-people-read-2017-7#elon-musk-8
https://science.howstuffworks.com/life/cellular-microscopic/does-body-really-replace-seven-years.htm
https://www.youtube.com/watch?v=xsA9llxuF00
https://www.youtube.com/watch?v=OqLT_CNTNYA
https://www.success.com/4-ways-to-actively-reprogram-your-thoughts/
https://en.wikiversity.org/wiki/Talk:Albert_Einstein_quote
https://www.goodreads.com/quotes/112594-thoughts-become-things-if-you-see-it-in-your-mind
https://www.nightingale.com/articles/the-myths-realities-of-achieving-financial-independence/
https://www.youtube.com/watch?v=cbjyMfwRCPA
https://allauthor.com/quotes/90095/
https://www.goodreads.com/quotes/1191114-the-sculpture-is-already-complete-within-the-marble-block-before
https://www.goodreads.com/quotes/321104-inch-by-inch-life-s-a-cinch-yard-by-yard-life-s
https://www.daveramsey.com/blog/what-is-the-fire-movement
https://www.jackcanfield.com/pages/the-success-principles-workbook-masterclass-replay/?utm_source=email&utm_medium=email&utm_c

Alpha Book Publisher

ampaign=tspworkbook&utm_content=masterclassreplay&inf_contact_key=e36643f451021e9e28c34376f591162 1a61f15688044e0df333a256a7a7fd2ca
https://www.youtube.com/watch?v=RBn_tqY-1Qw
https://www.getyourselfoptimized.com/living-life-values-dr-john-demartini/
http://www.djpetealexander.com/blog/2020/3/22/when-the-ego-weeps-for-what-it-has-lost-the-spirit-rejoices-for-what-it-has-found
https://www.youtube.com/watch?v=f1Zc7EYXdds
https://quotefancy.com/quote/1752734/Lewis-Gordon-There-is-nothing-more-powerful-than-the-made-up-mind
https://www.success.com/to-be-successful-burn-your-boats/
https://www.linkedin.com/pulse/understanding-analogy-chicken-pig-egg-bacon-breakfast-ananthalingam
https://www.skillshare.com/classes/Positive-Psychology-and-Philosophy-for-the-21st-Century/1035976473?via=search-layout-grid
https://somewhatfunny.com/quote/154
https://www.brainyquote.com/quotes/theodore_roosevelt_120663
https://en.wikipedia.org/wiki/Three_Wooden_Crosses
https://www.goodreads.com/quotes/227942-i-used-to-walk-down-the-street-like-i-was
https://www.youtube.com/watch?v=Pca24nzCdu0
https://www.countryliving.com/life/g28564406/gratitude-quotes/?slide=3
https://www.countryliving.com/life/g28564406/gratitude-quotes/?slide=4
https://www.countryliving.com/life/g28564406/gratitude-quotes/?slide=6

Alpha Book Publisher

https://www.skillshare.com/classes/Positive-Psychology-and-Philosophy-for-the-21st-Century/1035976473/projects?via=search-layout-grid
https://www.youtube.com/watch?v=NGbn-9eU7vg
https://www.reddit.com/r/inspiration/comments/ephxe4/develop_your_communication_skills_because_when/
https://www.youtube.com/watch?v=FfHjJ-vib_w
https://www.goodreads.com/quotes/3160-today-you-are-you-that-is-truer-than-true-there
https://en.wikipedia.org/wiki/Hicham_El_Guerrouj
https://en.wikipedia.org/wiki/Four-minute_mile
https://www.google.com/search?client=firefox-b-1-d&q=Happy+people+lyrics+little+big+town
https://www.brainyquote.com/quotes/maya_angelou_392897
https://www.goodreads.com/quotes/534889-the-mind-is-a-wonderful-servant-but-a-terrible-master
https://www.youtube.com/watch?v=G4ASwHif2U8
https://en.wikipedia.org/wiki/Dopamine
https://www.forbes.com/sites/daviddisalvo/2014/08/10/how-telling-the-truth-could-keep-you-healthier/#bfa0f043a8e4
https://ethicalleadership.nd.edu/news/what-dishonesty-does-to-your-brain-why-lying-becomes-easier-and-easier/
https://www.youtube.com/watch?v=CjOvWYcpRaU
https://medium.com/change-your-mind/how-gratitude-rewires-your-brain-and-how-to-make-it-work-for-you-894e8bf73c59
https://www.youtube.com/watch?v=q9CtSqgcVe4
https://www.espn.com/nba/story/_/id/26709944/inside-relationship-unleashed-steph-curry-greatness

Alpha Book Publisher

https://www.ksl.com/article/46506476/oprah-tells-utah-audience-that-your-legacy-is-every-life-you-touch
https://www.simplypsychology.org/maslow.html
https://www.mayoclinic.org/healthy-lifestyle/stress-management/in-depth/positive-thinking/art-20043950
https://www.nytimes.com/2017/09/19/well/mind/how-honesty-could-make-you-happier.html
https://www.shape.com/lifestyle/mind-and-body/your-brain-lying
https://www.youtube.com/watch?v=VYYXq1Ox4sk&feature=youtu.be
https://greatergood.berkeley.edu/article/item/5_ways_giving_is_good_for_you
https://time.com/collection/guide-to-happiness/4070299/secret-to-happiness/
https://bornthisway.foundation/
https://www.youtube.com/watch?v=vVSI1V2Tscw
https://www.wanderlustworker.com/whatever-the-mind-can-conceive-and-believe-it-can-achieve/
https://www.google.com/search?client=firefox-b-1-d&q=Winston+Churchill+the+truth+is+
https://www.youtube.com/watch?v=VLd5XKo1Nnk
https://www.goodreads.com/quotes/82410-my-creed-i-do-not-choose-to-be-a-common
https://www.brainyquote.com/quotes/les_brown_389885
https://www.goodreads.com/quotes/1188139-pain-is-temporary-it-may-last-for-a-minute-or
https://www.goodreads.com/quotes/13533-courage-is-being-scared-to-death-but-saddling-up-anyway
https://www.pinterest.com/pin/555702041493409820/
https://urbanbalance.com/the-story-of-two-wolves/
https://biblehub.com/proverbs/18-21.htm

Alpha Book Publisher

https://www.youtube.com/watch?v=X5nrZBrxdQ8
https://www.youtube.com/watch?v=VYYXq1Ox4sk&feature=youtu.be
https://www.youtube.com/watch?v=o5uUgbcK5KU&feature=youtu.be
https://www.biblegateway.com/passage/?search=Proverbs+29%3A18&version=KJV
https://www.youtube.com/watch?v=ywuse55qU2A
https://www.youtube.com/watch?v=_IpzpbGCvqY
https://www.positivelypresent.com/2010/09/7-benefits-of-being-openminded.html
http://operationmeditation.com/discover/8-benefits-of-having-an-open-mind-and-how-to-get-one/
https://www.conehealth.com/services/behavioral-health/4-health-benefits-of-giving-to-others-/
https://www.youtube.com/watch?v=7bB_fVDlvhc
https://positivepsychology.com/daily-affirmations/
https://www.youtube.com/watch?v=kJk1eGXMK18
https://www.psychologytoday.com/us/blog/prescriptions-life/201803/how-stop-comparing-yourself-others
https://www.rush.edu/health-wellness/discover-health/health-benefits-giving
https://www.goodreads.com/quotes/71-the-fool-doth-think-he-is-wise-but-the-wise
https://paulaowens.com/power-words/
https://www.youtube.com/watch?v=Gzj7zP5BXdc&feature=youtu.be
https://fortune.com/2016/08/08/billionaires-no-degree/
https://www.lifehack.org/articles/productivity/10-common-excuses-that-lead-you-nowhere-success.html
https://www.lifehack.org/articles/productivity/10-common-excuses-that-lead-you-nowhere-success.html

https://www.brainyquote.com/quotes/maya_angelou_392897

https://iarp.org/chakra-basics/

https://www.pinterest.com/pin/362962051200680790/

https://positivepsychology.com/positive-psychology-quotes/

https://www.azquotes.com/quote/543413

https://www.skillshare.com/classes/Using-Design-Psychology-to-Maximize-Creativity-at-Home-and-Work/454611310/projects?

Alpha Book Publisher

Alpha Book Publisher

Made in the USA
Monee, IL
10 January 2023